TO BE CHRISTIAN

TO BE CHRISTIAN

The surpassing worth of knowing Jesus

GRAEME SCHULTZ

Gobsmacked Publishing

All Scripture quotations, unless otherwise indicated, are taken from the Holy Bible, New International Version®, NIV®. Copyright ©1973, 1978, 1984, 2011 by Biblica, Inc.™ Used by permission of Zondervan. All rights reserved worldwide. www.zondervan.com The "NIV" and "New International Version" are trademarks registered in the United States Patent and Trademark Office by Biblica, Inc.™

Copyright © 2019 by Graeme Schultz.

All rights reserved. No part of this publication may be reproduced, distributed or transmitted in any form or by any means, including photocopying, recording, or other electronic or mechanical methods, without the prior written permission of the publisher, except in the case of brief quotations embodied in critical reviews and certain other non-commercial uses permitted by copyright law. For permission requests, write to the publisher, addressed "Permissions Coordinator," at the address below.

Graeme Schultz/Gobsmacked Publishing

19 Trotters Lane
Cudgee, Victoria, Australia, 3265

Email: graeme@design2build.net.au

www.gobsmackedpublishing.com.au

Cataloguing-in-Publication Data:

Author: Schultz, Graeme

Email: graeme@design2build.net.au

Title: TO BE CHRISTIAN

Subjects: Devotional

TO BE CHRISTIAN

Graeme Schultz

ISBN 978-0-6484690-4-9 (paperback)
ISBN 978-0-6484690-5-6 (e-book)

Typeset by bookbound.com.au

Contents

Introduction		vii
CHAPTER 1	Diversity	1
CHAPTER 2	On Being Good	5
CHAPTER 3	Charity	9
CHAPTER 4	Pizza	13
CHAPTER 5	Reason	17
CHAPTER 6	The Broad Church And The Narrow Way	20
CHAPTER 7	The Gospel Of Death	23
CHAPTER 8	All In A Good Cause	27
CHAPTER 9	To Know Christ	30
CHAPTER 10	The God Who Is Love	33
CHAPTER 11	Superstition	37
CHAPTER 12	Supernatural	40
CHAPTER 13	Feeding On Christ	44
CHAPTER 14	Crucified With Christ	48
CHAPTER 15	The Pizza Of Self	52
CHAPTER 16	The Popular Mix	55
CHAPTER 17	Knowing Christ	58
CHAPTER 18	Resting In Love	62
CHAPTER 19	God's Toppings	66
CHAPTER 20	The Competence Of The Spirit	70

CHAPTER 21	To Be Christian	73
CHAPTER 22	To Have Christ	76
CHAPTER 23	Will The Real Graeme Please Stand Up	80
CHAPTER 24	Extravagance	84
CHAPTER 25	Wildest Dreams	89

Introduction

To be Christian has become a very unspecific thing.

The familiar term 'a broad church' might well be applied to the Christian community itself, we have become so wide ranging and all-encompassing that it's quite difficult to pin down who and what we actually are, (or aren't).

The church has, in effect, become a reflection of humanity – and the diversity, opinions, causes and purposes observed in the wider world have become reflected in the church too, with the result that it's difficult to nail down what the word 'Christian' means anymore.

Its philosophical diversity has made the church into such a vast collection of causes, charities, institutions, communities, persuasions, expressions and values, that determining what is actually 'Christian', and what only looks like 'Christian' has become an impossible task.

The statement "if it looks like a duck and quacks like a duck – it must be a duck" can no longer be applied to the church, because we don't actually know what a duck should look like anymore. Ducks have some unique characteristics: they swim, they fly, they quack, they look cute... but taken in isolation, any one of these characteristics could be applied to a range of other creatures. Similarly, Christians can't be recognised by their isolated characteristics either.

Take charity, for instance; we know that there are many charitable causes and institutions within the Christian context, but does the expression of charity necessarily imply that one is Christian? Many who demonstrate charitable actions are not claiming to be Christian, so charity in itself is not a useful measure of our Christianity.

Or perhaps spirituality? A distinctly spiritual characteristic exists within the church which ranges from the subdued to the outwardly demonstrative, but many outside the church are now also laying claim to the term 'spiritual' – to the extent that it is no longer only a religious term, but also a term embraced by a secular society.

Even atheists have laid claim to their own version of spirituality which springs from an inner enlightenment and awareness of a universal energy, but does not actually relate to any deity or God. Others have borrowed from various religions and philosophies to compile their own unique hybrid, linking ideas that they find compelling together to form a spirituality unique to them.

It's not unusual these days to believe in a religious concept like reincarnation without actually being religious; it's just a matter of putting reincarnation into our personal spiritual mix alongside other things like crystals, auras or whatever takes our fancy.

And the same can be said of Christianity. We can embrace just about anything we like, as long as we can give it a vaguely spiritual label and live in harmony with our particular community .

It's possible to be Christian these days without actually knowing God.

Some find this diversity pleasing because it embraces the wide-ranging differences within humanity – so the individuality and uniqueness of each person and group is encouraged as the true expression of the multi-faceted nature of the human race.

Personally though, I find it troubling that we have become so tolerant of this spiritual versatility; it concerns me that in being tolerant, we have lost sight of who we really are.

But who are we?

That is the point of this book – what is it that makes us Christian? And in contrast, what is simply our unique personal expression of life?

From a purely human perspective, diversity is able to be embraced and applauded; but if God is the true Supreme Being He claims to be, then we must ultimately conform to His truth. If not, we will perpetuate the notion that Adam first devised, that we can be our own self-oriented god – *while also acknowledging another more divine God.*

Adam was the first to diversify. He added another layer to give expression to his unique makeup and decided to run two truths side by side – the ultimate fact of who God is along with the more general expression of his own unique self. Adam attempted to blend his own point of view with God's, so that what began as a very specific truth was broadened to accommodate Adam's individuality.

Religion was born, and the comfortable mixing of opinions was the result.

In effect, Adam decided that he wanted life to work differently from the way God had set it up; he wanted to have a say on the board and contribute his point of view into the mix, and man-generated spirituality in all its forms is the outcome of Adam's decision.

This diversity of opinion may seem relatively benign if it were limited to those who are professing spirituality outside of Christ, but it becomes seriously problematic when it infiltrates and redefines the church itself.

So the issue before us is not whether we should express our Christianity in a variety of ways, but whether our Christianity is fundamentally about our unique personal expression at all.

Now you're scaring me!

Don't panic, I'm not suggesting that our life choices are not important; rather, the point is that something even higher and greater than our individual expression exists that we may have missed amidst all the clutter of going about our Christianity, and until we discover it, we remain trapped in Adam's choice.

Adam walked away from the best part.

As we go along, we will examine the different ways we have embraced Adam's choice at the expense of God's best – we will attempt to get a handle on how the new mode of operation that Adam chose for us has played out in the wider Christian context, and what we have been missing as a result.

You might see yourself in some of the scenarios – I did; and the idea of reconsidering things may seem a bit confronting – but strap yourself in, and take a deep breath, and let's see if there is more to this whole Christian thing than we first might have thought.

CHAPTER 1

Diversity

Imagine yourself as a pizza.

For some that might be a challenge, for others – *not so much*.

Pizzas have a mix of toppings, a diverse collection of ingredients which make the pizza what it is – and we also are a collection of all the ingredients that have been placed onto us during our life.

These ingredients have been placed onto us by our upbringing, our personality, the relationships and experiences we have had, the influential people in our life, and the values of the wider community. These ingredients (or toppings) are unique to us and to a large extent we didn't choose them – they were simply placed onto us by life. And even now, they continue to be added to us on a daily basis.

We might think that we are a pure, untainted representation of humanity, and that our unique makeup is self-determined; but that is not really the case. We are actually the product of all of the influences that have formed us thus far – both good and bad.

And it is even more complicated than that; genetic factors were assigned to us before we were even born. We had no say in them; they were randomly placed on to us by the forces at play at the time and added to us without our permission. Some go all the way back to Adam, toppings which are as ancient as the human race itself have landed on us and influence who we are now – what makes up the pizza of 'me' is a very complicated mix of ingredients indeed.

So what? There's nothing wrong with being a unique individual.

True, our individuality is to be celebrated, but this unique mix also has a downside; it determines our unique version of reality, which extends all the way into our perception of God.

Inadvertently, we know God on the basis of all that has formed us thus far. The God we know is actually the sum total of all of the things that have been placed onto us by life. For a Christian, those influences have possibly come from family, church, ministry, theology and a myriad of casual conversations and experiences collected over a lifetime within the great big machine we call Christianity.

And those experiences and conversations have in turn been fine-tuned by the innate, long-term values we hold that have been inextricably wired into us by our upbringing. We are a very unique mix of such a diversity of conscious and subconscious influences – *yet inside our own head, we are normal.*

And from this mixed bag we endeavour to produce a view of God which is pure and true.

I'm not suggesting that our big picture understanding of God is necessarily tainted, but rather that our day-to-day living out of our faith in God is as much the sum of all that life has placed onto us thus far, as it is the truth about us from God's perspective.

> **In other words we are more likely to be defined by the best and worst that life has handed us, than the magnificence of the love union we share with our Heavenly Father.**

For example, I have a dear friend who suffered for a long time through a very abusive marriage. Though she is a Christian and believes deeply in God's love for her, she sees herself more from the perspective of being a victim of abuse than from her status as the recipient of God's unsearchable love. The ingredient of abuse which was added to her life is completely overshadowed by the extravagance of her Heavenly Father's love for her, yet the abuse she suffered continues to define her and her life – including her perception of God.

I have another friend who grew up under a violent father who bashed his brother, his mother, and him on a daily basis. He never understood love and self-destructed his own marriage years later because of it. His mother was a believer who passed on her faith in God to her sons, but my friend became a man more defined by violence than love because its self-defining influence was placed upon him. Now, many years later, he is at last discovering how to love and be loved as he embraces a new perspective of God.

Both of my friends were held captive for many years by the influence that was placed onto them against their own will – they had no choice in the matter – and they inadvertently formed God out of the stuff that life had handed to them.

These are extreme and very negative examples and go to illustrate the potential for the ingredients that life has placed onto us to influence our view of life in general and God in particular.

Yet it's not restricted to negative influences. In fact, positive influences can have as much potential to create a distorted image of God as negative ones – when those positive influences emphasise the potential for good in humanity, rather than the absence of good in all of us without the life-giving work of Christ.

Think about that!

That is the defining fact of the Tree of the Knowledge of Good and Evil which Adam chose for humanity back in the beginning. It influences us to value human behaviour above the freely given gift of life that flows from the heart of God, and in so doing, it redefines Christianity to be more about our lifestyle than God's love.

In other words, the problem we face as we attempt to construct the truth out of all the toppings that have been placed on us by life, is that we are more likely to form a view of God which places Him somewhere within all the good and evil we have experienced – rather than viewing God as one who independently loves us and gives us life, in spite of all the good and evil.

God designed humankind to be influenced by one topping only, His extravagant outpouring of love – an influence which enables us to walk through life with such peace and confidence that all the good and evil has no power to control us. Yet, Adam opted for a man-centric alternative that has been defining and limiting humanity ever since.

> *This redefining of humanity is the real problem*
> *– we don't know who we really are.*
> *And because we don't know who we are,*
> *we don't know who God is.*

In the chapters that follow, we will look at the toppings that life has placed upon humanity. We will attempt to wade through the sludge of life and get back up onto the dry land of God's pure, undefiled love.

From this high ground, we will cast our gaze over the truth as God sees it, a truth which is so radically different from the one handed to us by Adam that it bears no comparison.

It is a reality that is so superior to the one placed upon us by life that it has the capacity to transform us back into our original design – a design which puts the self-defining role back in our own hands. No longer are we subject to the random influences of life, but are now able to recalibrate those influences into subjection to the greatest truth of all, that we are the objects of God's extravagant love.

CHAPTER 2

On Being Good

Life shapes us and, as a consequence, how we perceive God and His expression on the earth. To get a handle on this we need to rethink our view of 'good'.

In Mark 10:18, when Jesus was approached by a man who called Him 'good teacher', He responded with an unlikely reply. "Why do you call me good?" Jesus answered. "No one is good, except God alone".

We know that Jesus was God, so surely that was sufficient for Him to lay claim to the 'good' tag – but apparently not, and Jesus gives us the explanation in John 5:26, "For as the Father has life in Himself, so He has granted the Son to have life in Himself".

Jesus needed to be in union with His Father for the dynamic life He expressed on earth to be present in His life, without that union He was no different to the rest of us. And that was the problem with Adam, he wanted to produce his own goodness quite apart from the goodness that was granted to him by God… and the fallen nature of humanity was born.

So, the rethinking of our view of 'good' is more about its source than its earthly expression – "no one is good but God alone". Even Jesus stepped back from assuming 'goodness' as an inherent characteristic He possessed and declared that it was actually a characteristic that was applied to Him as He shared in His love union with His Father.

It is not my intention to diminish the goodness of Jesus in the reader's mind, but rather to shine the light on the capacity of the extravagant love of God to grant goodness to all of us as we rest in our Heavenly Father's generous gift of divine life. There is no question that Jesus was good; it is an undisputable fact. It is the source of that goodness which has eluded us. Jesus knew how to rest in His Father's love, and goodness overflowed through Him from that restful union.

This is a clear illustration of the events that took place in the Garden of Eden. Adam disconnected Himself from the Tree of Life and chose to be nourished by the Tree of the Knowledge of Good and Evil. He chose a diet for humanity that depended upon his own generation of goodness, rather than the free gift of goodness which was granted to him as he rested in God's love. Adam redefined humanity as a race of people stuck in the cycle of self-generating their own goodness, when God's original design had us receiving the goodness of God directly from His heart as we rested in His desire to grant it to us for free.

This is one of the first toppings that was ever placed upon humanity, and it has been reinforced by life ever since – that the human expression of goodness (in all its forms) is the point of our Christianity.

Jesus reacted quite strongly to the notion that He could 'be' good. Goodness was not something that He did; instead, it was something that defined His being because of the union He shared with His Father.

So in rethinking goodness it is important that we see it the same way Jesus did. It begins at the source and can only be expressed as the overflow of that source, which is the love of God.

Adam thought he could create a new source (the heart of man), but that is not true goodness; it is merely a collection of man-generated actions, which are nothing more than a shadow of true goodness. The cycle of self-made goodness, which now defines humanity, has kept us from a form of goodness which is radically superior yet effectively lost from our view by the clamour of our altruistic urge to present God with our personal best, instead of spontaneously allowing His best to fill and energize us as we were first designed.

The topping labelled 'be your best' has obscured our view of something dramatically superior: we can be God's best as we rest in His love.

You might be thinking, "What's wrong with human goodness?" – and the answer is nothing, but we must not value it above its true worth. Human beings showing each other acts of kindness and respect is indeed a noble thing, but Adam elevated human goodness to a level for which it was never intended – that it would define our worth and become the source of our being.

For that, only the gift of God's love would suffice.

And therein lies the dilemma of a large segment of Christianity. We know that goodness is important, and so we set about self-generating it just like Adam did, instead of discovering the radiant extravagance of God's love and learning how to have it restfully flow through us.

Who would have thought that a topping which is so defining of Christianity could be limiting us to the best of Adam, when the best of Jesus is available to us.

Paul addressed this in the book of Galatians when he challenged the church about their dependence on the practice of circumcision. Nothing was wrong with circumcision; in fact, it offered health benefits that were important in that time and place in history. However, it had become a pivotal part of their identity and sense of worth – and for that only the love expressed at the cross of Jesus would do.

Christians have been doing it ever since, inserting their behaviour and lifestyle or religious practices, in front of (or as a condition for receiving) God's freely given and unconditional gift of life. We have chosen the good ahead of the best – all because we don't realise that the best is an option that is truly available to us.

The toppings that have been placed on us have called forth something from us that God doesn't want – the best of Adam; He wants us to present to Him the best of His own indwelling Spirit.

Let's not make the mistake of thinking that Adam was a bad guy. He was in fact the best version of man to ever walk the planet as far as it relates to human qualities, but God didn't want him to live a life that drew upon his own resources to shape a life of worth. For that, only the virtue that overflowed from the heart of God would do.

Am I suggesting that God doesn't want us to live a virtuous life? Not at all. But I am suggesting that we must recalibrate the value we place on human virtue, because it is keeping us from the very best there is – God's nature dwelling in humankind.

"But can't I have both?" you ask.

You can if you like, but that question implies that the scale of the alternative offered to us by God is not clear to you. This is not a question about the importance and value of living a good and decent life; that is a given. It is about whether God views human virtue in the same way we do, and whether we were created to operate from His point of view or ours.

> **It all comes down to the cross of Christ,
> why we think Christ came,
> and how we perceive the outcomes of His death and resurrection.**

If all Jesus intended was that He provide us with a free pardon from our sins and a useful example of how to live a godly life, then by all means we should make it our life's work to strive to live the most virtuous life possible. But if Jesus died to crucify the self-made security of humanity so that the failed legacy of Adam could make way for the life of the Spirit, then we are facing a completely different issue. The first one attempts to re-energise the sagging efforts of Adam, and the second one kills Adam's way to make way for the indwelling Spirit of God.

...this is especially difficult for good people.

CHAPTER 3
Charity

I am not referring to just the charity that comes out of charitable organizations, but all forms of charity, both structured and spontaneous. Christianity has been defined by it for centuries, and we do a fine job of it to a large extent.

It recent decades, that charity has extended to the environment and the planet we call home. We have become a broad church of the socially aware: the need is great, the plight of the human race is evident everywhere, and we have responded with a new branch of Christianity called Social Responsibility.

We have no shortage of worthy causes, ranging from feeding the starving nations and the homeless on our own shores, to saving endangered species and closing the hole in the ozone layer – but is that supposed to be what defines us?

I'm not suggesting that these causes are not worthy of our effort and energy, but does our participation in these social causes actually make us Christian? It's not a question of need, or a question of our involvement in meeting that need, but a question of whether or not our involvement in such causes should validate us and provide us with our sense of Christian worth and identity.

If our involvement in social causes provides for our sense of identity as Christians, then we have become nothing more than a sophisticated version of Adam that finds our meaning in the best of human effort, above our place as the objects of God's freely given love.

If you think I'm being too harsh, then please accept that I am not trying to diminish the value of good works or the people who have given their lives in the pursuit of them, but rather that I am saying that good works do not set Christians apart from the herd. Good and bad exist everywhere.

Only the life of the indwelling Spirit of God can set us apart... *otherwise, why be Christian at all?*

I guess that last statement clarifies the problem.

It is so easy to be attached to the wrong things. We want to be Christian, and in the absence of a compelling view of the work that Jesus accomplished on the cross, we continue to choose to be defined by the nature of Adam that made it necessary in the first place.

> **We want Christianity,**
> **but we don't know how to find Christ.**

So we relegate Him to 'example' status and get on with the *job* of Christianity, instead of losing ourselves in the *person* of Christianity.

This situation becomes painfully evident when Christians find it easier to talk about their cause, program or charity than Jesus himself. There is a disconnect, almost an awkwardness, as if Jesus is a concept lost in history rather than the indwelling Spirit who gives us life for every moment of every day.

But what else can we expect of a form of Christianity that honours (dare I say, worships) the efforts of humanity above the indwelling life of Christ, all because we don't know it is a serious alternative for us.

So, what about the truly generous-hearted servants among us – the selfless ones who serve without the need or desire for recognition? Where do they fit in?

As I said earlier, this is not an examination of whether service or charity are honourable pursuits, but rather, that without the indwelling Spirit of God these pursuits are constrained within Adam's world system. Good people deserve honour, but that earth-based honour is not the honour for which we were first designed and subsequently remade by the blood of Jesus.

> **We were designed for the honour**
> **of walking around the Spirit of God.**

I mentioned earlier that this is especially difficult for good people – those who have perhaps been defined for a lifetime by doing good, serving and giving. It's hard to imagine any improvement to the best of humanity.

So the point is not to dishonour the best we can do as good people living out our days on earth, but to re-value the possibility of walking around the heart and nature of God.

I mean *really* walking around the heart and nature of God, not just repeating the words as a pleasing Christian cliché.

This is where the rubber meets the road. It has been a very long time since Christianity as a whole has been *primarily* defined by the indwelling Spirit of God, so it comes out of left field to be told that we as a collective community have been missing out on the best part. Instead, His indwelling has been a side issue we accepted theologically, but by which we are not personally defined.

My own experience has been that holding a theological point of view or embracing the language of Christianity without being personally redefined by that truth does not have the ability to transform me. I must choose to make that truth the life-defining fact of my existence, or else it will simply sit in the theological folder that I only go to for reference purposes.

So the fact of the matter is that I am no better off than a charitable non-Christian (even if I am the most charitable Christian on the planet) if I have not chosen the work of Christ as the primary fact that defines me.

How do we make the work of Christ our life-defining truth?

The only way to do that is to spend time at the cross asking God what it was all about, and what took place there that effects who I am – n*ot what I do, but who I am.*

The cross of Christ is more than an historic event; it is as real today as it was 2,000 years ago, and we can go there in refection and prayer and ask God anything. It is the connection between us and His love for humanity. He delights to tell us what it was really all about.

You may find that, like me, you get some answers you didn't expect. My faith had been so neatly contained within the lifestyle and religious activities of Christianity that I was quite surprised to find that none of that stuff seemed to register very highly in God's mind. It was more about what He had done for me than what I could do for Him or for humankind.

That's the scandalous thing about the cross of Christ; it sets us back to our original design, and the first casualty is our attachment to our own self-motivated and self-managed lives. Even really good things like church attendance, prayer, Bible reading and raising a Christian family must be the overflow of discovering that God is already completely happy with us as we place faith in Jesus – and that anything that overflows from *that* fact is just the icing on the cake.

I didn't understand any of that by contemplating the value of my good works. I had to pull my attention off myself and on to Christ for the scale and magnificence of my salvation to finally dawn on me. While I was preoccupied with myself, my response to God, and my management of life, I couldn't grasp the staggering accomplishment that Christ completed in me and for me on the cross.

At first it seemed that by shifting my focus away from my good lifestyle I was devaluing all that was important in Christianity; but eventually, after I settled down and let God show me the truth, I discovered the opposite to be true. By fixing my eyes on Jesus, I was truly valuing my Christianity. I saw then that His sacrifice was so brilliant compared to my puny attempts to present God with my pleasing life, that it eclipsed my self-effort altogether.

And in eclipsing it, I discovered the real truth
– He is better at being me than I am.

CHAPTER 4
Pizza

A few days ago, we had some of our family over to celebrate Father's Day. Some of our children and grandchildren who live locally popped in to share a meal and the fun that comes with creating our own pizzas.

I dusted off my old pizza oven and set it up on the deck while Angela prepared the dough for the pizza bases. The whole kitchen bench was required for the activity, and a vast selection of toppings in individual containers was laid out in readiness for our guests. Ham, salami, bacon, chicken, mushrooms, olives, onion, dried tomatoes, pineapple, capsicum, cheese, tomato paste, and a selection of herbs and spices were all laid out in readiness.

Then the gang arrived and more ingredients were added to the already overflowing bench top.

The grandchildren kicked off the party, flour on the round wooden board, then a lump of dough – roll it out till it fills the board, spread the tomato paste and begin adding the toppings.

Making pizzas is a messy business; flour is not easily contained (especially by 3 year olds), containers of ingredients were accidently bumped off the bench, and the dough had a mind of its own – but before long, the first pizza appeared.

It was not the most ambitious pizza ever made, erring on the side of caution to agree with the milder palate of the children, but it was a triumph nonetheless – and devoured in minutes.

As we went along, those who considered themselves pizza connoisseurs began to create. Impossible combinations of ingredients began rolling off the production line and, against all likelihood, they tasted magnificent.

Those who were less adventurous relied on the tried and true combinations and copped a measure of sarcastic banter from the sophisticated gallery for their conservative approach – but in the end it was agreed that it all tasted spectacular, as attested by the fact that it was all eaten.

Angela prepared twelve lumps of dough, and we managed to use eleven of them. That's eleven pizzas among nine people – with only a few scraps and crusts left over to feed the chooks the next day.

The real challenge came at the end when the ingredients were running low – the challenge to create a gourmet pizza out of the slim pickings remaining in the containers. Dan rose to the challenge and created a pizza of extraordinary delicacy, which was more a combination of herbs, spices and culinary dexterity than all that had gone before – and it too was devoured by all as if it had been piled high with the first pickings.

It's obvious that I am telling you this story to illustrate a point.

Imagine yourself as a pizza.

What kind of pizza are you?

Ambitious, safe, creative, conservative, dependable, extravagant, bland – the options are endless.

It's easy to be distracted by the particular arrangement of toppings that give each of us our unique character. We are at home with ourselves and consider our unique blend to be just right – but I wonder if there is something more to a great pizza than just the toppings.

I'm talking about the pizza base of course, the bread onto which all of the toppings are placed.

Angela is often complimented for her bread making, and her pizza bases are no exception – ideal for rolling out to a nice thin layer, yet tasty and great for holding all the ingredients together. The universal ingredient to all pizzas is the base; it is the foundation upon which the pizza is built, yet it is often bypassed as simply a necessary way of supporting the real pizza, the toppings.

Similarly, the universal foundation upon which we build our faith is Jesus, the Bread of Life.

It is easy to dismiss Jesus as simply the base upon which our lives are built, a necessary foundation so we can get on with the more important business of constructing the tastiest, most creative life imaginable. We know that He is there and that He is important – but it's hard to get excited about the bread when the diversity of toppings pulls at us, each expressing its unique potential to satisfy and nourish, each clamouring for pride of place on the pizza which is me.

We discussed earlier the ingredients of goodness and charity; they certainly clamour for our attention, and no pizza would be complete without them. But they have a way of sidelining the only real and essential ingredient, the Bread of Life.

> ***Adam reoriented humanity to be distracted by the toppings,
> when God's original intention
> was that we would be fixated on the Bread.***

That's the compelling thing about toppings. They appeal to us and have a way of grasping centre stage in our lives, with the ultimate outcome that we inadvertently begin to construct our life pizza without the Bread at all… which leads to a very unsatisfactory pizza indeed.

It sounds ridiculous, doesn't it – building a pizza without bread? But I can tell you from personal experience that it is a very common practice amongst Christians. We talk about the Bread, and in our own way we value the Bread, but we don't actually know how to build our lives upon it – so we progress to the more compelling task of working on our toppings and relegate the Bread to theoretical status.

Building upon the Bread of Life is not simply a matter of going to church, praying and reading the Bible. If it were, then Adam would have been just fine. Instead it requires a re-evaluation of the cross of Christ such that we allow the work that was accomplished there to hold us and contain us, and that it is an end unto itself without the addition of any of life's toppings.

For much of my life, I perceived the cross of Christ as simply the framework that my life was built upon. It was the theological scaffolding that carried the important part – my toppings, the uniquely diverse mix of lifestyle and religious activities that gave expression to me.

But how wrong I was.

Jesus is my life; He is not my cause or my ministry or my area of service, and He is even more than my life support mechanism. He is, in fact, intrinsically the new me, and my toppings are irrelevant until I truly understand that.

It is the great reversal; I have gone from being all toppings, to being all Bread.

This is the work of the cross – that Christ accomplished something impossible in me. He took a man who was defined by the best that he could make out of all the toppings that were placed on him, and replaced those toppings (good and bad) with the best of heaven, the very life of God.

I can continue to value myself according to my management of life's toppings if I like, I can continue to be defined by the good that I make of it all – but there awaits a life that is so sublimely better if I will shift my gaze across to the staggering thing that Christ accomplished in me on the cross.

It is a matter of perspective; Adam had us fix our eyes on our unique self-management of life, and Jesus offers us a Spirit-managed life. Adam's option is very compelling. We are attracted to a life focussed on making the most out of our unique mix – but the life of the Spirit is our true design.

We were made to live in the Bread of Life.

CHAPTER 5

Reason

We are living in the age of reason; everything must pass through the test of logic before we can embrace it as fact.

Reason is a topping; it is a way of managing life. Some people are more reason-directed than others, but in the end we all come under its spell to some degree, either directly through our own thought processes or indirectly as we are influenced by others.

It is not that reason is a bad thing, but simply that some things, especially spiritual things, are beyond reason. If the unique makeup of our personality is strongly leaning towards reason, then we will be more inclined to try to get the supernatural things of God to fit into the natural explanations of life on earth.

On a very simplistic level, we might conduct a logical examination of Noah's ark and determine that it was reasonably capable of carrying the requisite number of animals and their food and waste requirements, etc. But if something cannot be logically explained, then we are more likely to relegate it to the category of embellishment or metaphor, rather than embrace it at face value.

I'm not referring in particular to the usual debate about the six day creation or the story of Jonah in the belly of the fish, but the Bible teachings that are more easily dismissed as creative illustrations rather than actual realities.

Take Paul's statement in Galatians 2:20, "I have been crucified with Christ". Clearly his body wasn't crucified with Christ as it was still engaged in the process of writing to the Galatians, so the voice of reason relegates such a statement to the category of metaphor – but in so doing, the magnificence of Christ's work is normalised and loses its transformative power.

The voice of reason within the Christian community is yet another broad church that has established itself so completely among us that we can't imagine Christianity without it. It makes sense to apply intellectual reasoning on some level to all facets of life, and the church has been caught up in it as well. Just like charity, it fits us so well that we can't imagine being Christian without it.

I'm not advocating ignorance or dim-wittedness. Quite to the contrary, I am advocating something much higher than human reasoning, not lower. I am suggesting that there is a beauty and balance to the Kingdom of God and the ways of the Holy Spirit, which is far better and comparatively more sensible than human logic… but it operates in an entirely different way.

The topping of human reasoning looks for physical proof to give validity to spiritual things, whereas the mind of Christ is not at all limited by the evidence on the ground. The mind of Christ locks on to the heart and nature of our Father God; it looks to the invisible realm of God's love to determine the facts, and then it proceeds to live boldly from that perspective.

That is not the way of thinking we inherited from Adam.

Remember in Genesis 3 where Adam and Eve realized for the first time that they were naked. They had been naked all along, but the reality of it only came into view when they looked away from the unconditional acceptance of God – to the conditional performance of their conduct in the natural realm. God hadn't changed; all that had changed was that Adam and Eve used human reasoning to determine a spiritual truth.

And now Jesus has returned to us the spiritual sight that Adam knew in the very beginning; the eyes of our hearts have been opened once again. This new enlightenment comes as we view the cross of Christ afresh and determine that it successfully turned back the clock – we have been returned to the garden of God's eternal pleasure where it all began, and the self-destruction caused by Adam and Eve has been made right again by the blood of Jesus.

None of that can be gained by human reasoning; it is a truth that relegates the thinking of Adam to the category of insanity. The human race has been temporarily insane for the millennia between Adam and Jesus, and now a new kind of sanity is available to us again called 'the mind of Christ' – but we must choose it if we want to walk in the Spirit.

It is up to us to take off the topping of human reasoning and take on the mind of Christ if we are to be truly Christian. That's why the Bible refers to Jesus as a stumbling block; we cannot grasp the life He came to give us, if we apply the mind of Adam to lay hold of the ways of the Spirit. So we stumble over this truth.

It seems so unthinkably wrong to go against the voice of human reason, and in so doing,
we live as only a fraction of the person that we actually are.

That's the problem with the toppings that have been placed upon us; they seem so right that we can't imagine life without them. And that is the challenge for each one of us who wishes to be truly Christian; we must take the radical step of entrusting our entire existence into the safety of God's love.

We can't just say the words and hope that everything will be okay. Rather, we must conduct such a thorough examination of the claims made by the cross of Christ that we surrender our very being into the fidelity of His love.

The topping of human reasoning won't go there, so a hybrid form of Christianity persists in many circles which embraces Christianity as a religious and lifestyle ideal, but does not entrust itself into Christ Himself.

Cherry-picking the bits of Christianity that best suit us is actually no Christianity at all; it might quack like a duck… *but that is the end of the comparison.*

CHAPTER 6
The Broad Church And The Narrow Way

The definition of a *broad church* is *"a group or doctrine which allows for and caters to a wide range of opinions and people"*.

It's not surprising that the church is as diverse as it is when you consider the range of opinions that it embraces. It contains the full range of persuasions from the most conservative to the most liberal, and pretty much everything in between.

A broad church by definition caters to a wide range of opinions and people, but I wonder if that is how the church should be. I wonder if we should cater to a wide range of people, but not a wide range of opinions.

I guess it comes down to our view of what the church is.

If it is a community that focusses on providing a safe environment of acceptance and tolerance and a doctrine that embraces the diverse opinions of all, then we should indeed settle for the definition above – we should claim the title of *broad church* and get on with the job of helping people to manage life and be happy.

> *But if the church is not that,*
> *if it is a narrow way,*
> *then it is not diversely opinioned at all*
> *– just diversely populated.*

The difference lies in the solution that the church offers to humanity.

A broad church offers humanity tolerance and the acceptance of a wide range of views. As such, its solution to humanity is unspecific; it just accepts every one where they are at.

The narrow way offers humanity intolerance and the rejection of a wide range of views. It is intolerant of humanity's expectation that God will accept them on their own terms (that was Adam's way), and it offers the life of Jesus instead. It rejects the diversity of human opinion and declares that no one comes to the Father but by Jesus.

The broad church and the narrow way are poles apart.

The broad church values the pizza toppings; the bread is merely a useful base to support them.

The narrow way values the pizza base; the diversity of toppings is meaningless without it.

In recent times, as the church has become more modernized and sophisticated, we have embraced the broad church way of thinking and taken on board the mantra of the wider world – tolerance and acceptance has become our catch cry. The message of Jesus has been re-defined to 'example' status, and we have joined the great community of humanity in embracing every opinion under the sun.

I heard a well-known Christian leader say recently that being Christian depends entirely on where you were born, and if you were born in a place that embraced another faith, then that faith would do just as well in connecting you to God. In his tolerance of diverse opinions, he was watering down the unique capacity of the blood of Jesus to save us. He was promoting the good (tolerance) at the expense of the best (redemption).

> *Jesus was tolerant of people but not of opinions.*
> *He ate with the tax collectors, prostitutes and sinners*
> *– but He refused to validate their misguided thinking.*

Modern Christianity seems to be having some difficulty with this differentiation. We seem to have drifted into the notion that there are no absolutes, and so, in tolerating all people, we must also cater to their opinions.

The ultimate outcome of this approach is that our tolerance becomes the gospel message instead of the salvation message of Jesus. We attempt to save people by accepting them ourselves, instead of leading them to the acceptance that was brokered for them at the cross of Christ.

So we take the example of Jesus (He ate with sinners) and go about replicating His acceptance as our primary purpose, instead of taking the blood of Jesus and leading people to repent of all their diverse opinions, so that they can embrace the unconditional love of God.

> *In reducing Jesus to mere example status,*
> *we become the saviour instead of Jesus.*

This rationalizing of the gospel is the result of the church categorizing Jesus as a message rather than a person. If He is a message, we can embrace it and replicate it in our own way; if He is a person, we are confronted with His wild claim that He wants us to die so He can move in and replace us.

The claims of Jesus are just too 'out there' for a *sensible* Christian institution to embrace; we have been conditioned by the thinking of Adam to expect a far more reasonable, all encompassing, man-energized solution to the plight of humanity – so we settle for tolerance instead of death.

And miss out on the best part.

CHAPTER 7

The Gospel Of Death

Who wants to die before their time – *not me!*

However, the apostle Paul, who was a one of the world's great wordsmiths, frequently used the term *death* to describe the normal experience of the believer.

"I have been crucified with Christ, I no longer live but Christ lives in me". (Galatians 2:20)

"For you died, and your life is now hidden with Christ in God". (Colossians 3:3)

"One died for all, therefore all died". (2 Corinthians 5:15)

Paul was not a closet masochist or aspiring martyr who relished the notion of death; it wasn't like that at all. He was describing the actual process of being Christian. Nor was he suggesting that this death is something we undertake ourselves by daily subjugating our most base human impulses – this was a spiritual death, brought on by receiving the work of the cross.

We cannot be Christian without embracing this death.

Modern Christianity wants to keep us alive by catering to our diverse opinions and lifestyles, but in so doing it does us the most unimaginably tragic disservice – it keeps us from the new life which is our true design. In attempting to show kindness, we are actually robbed of God's best for us and offered nothing more than a modernization of Adam's folly.

I know what I am talking about. I spent 55 years of my life wandering around in the wilderness of Adam's well-intentioned version of Christianity – it was all that was on offer, and I did my best to make it work. I kept alive the family legacy handed to me by old grandpa Adam, when I should have seen it for what it was – a failed man-made system that had been replaced by the real thing, 'Christ in me'.

This old system was based on one thing – that there is something in humanity inherently good, and all we have to do is bring it to the surface. We do this by encouraging people to be their best, to be a bit kinder to each other and a bit less selfish, and if we follow the example of Jesus, everything will turn out fine and we will live happily ever after.

It came as a shock to me to discover that (from God's perspective) there is nothing good in us, and the best way forward is to hand the self-capacity of Adam over to God so that it can join Christ and be crucified, allowing a brand new spirit-man to be born.

'Nothing good in us' – this is a very politically incorrect gospel indeed.

You see the old man must die before the new man can be born; else we perpetuate the very problem that Jesus came to fix.

If the gospel we embrace is that humanity can be fixed by a process of behavioural modification and self-improvement, then we don't really need Jesus at all. All we need is new teaching, better exampling of a life well lived, and a lot of self-help books and programs that demonstrate a more loving way to relate to each other.

But Jesus didn't see it that way and decided to scrap the whole thing.

Are you shocked?

Does it disturb you to think that the gospel of love could be so intolerant of us, and that this love can so easily discard us to the scrap heap? Surely there must be something worth keeping, something of virtue in the combined inventory of human goodness which would merit saving from the fate of the scrap heap.

That's the thing about God's love; it is so great and so passionate about giving us the best, that it will not allow us to remain self-dependent (no matter how good we think it might look).

If we consider virtue as the basis of human altruism alone, then it is easy to assign value and potential to us. As I mentioned at the beginning of this book, there are many causes and programs of worth which people all over the world are engaged in to improve the lot of the needy and the environment around us. But God doesn't measure our worth on the basis of our contribution to society and nature; He measures it on the basis of His divine nature, which is so blazing in its perfection and so extravagantly life-giving, that human goodness doesn't even touch it. So it's not about whether human virtue is of any worth, but whether that worth is relevant in the eternal scheme of things.

By all means, we should be involved in any and every charitable and altruistic endeavour available to us, but not to the extent that they become the defining truth of the Christian faith – for that, only the unconditional love of God expressed upon the cross will do.

We were designed to lean in to the perfect nature of God. We were created to be carriers of His perfect image. We were conceived to be the objects of His perfect love. It is impossible for such a love to leave us floundering in the imperfections of the nature that Adam handed to us; God cannot do it and remain true to Himself.

He had no alternative but to save us from ourselves.

The challenge for us is this: "Do we want to be saved from something to which we are so attached?"

We are in the same boat that Adam was; the innate capacity within us to self-manage is so attractive that it's hard to imagine life any other way. So we stand before the two trees just like Adam did, looking from one to the other and weighing up the pros and cons. Will we choose life in the Spirit and dependence on God as the source of our life, or will we choose life in the flesh and our own independent self-management of life as our source?

Adam chose wrongly,
and Jesus has given us back the ability to choose all over again.

Adam chose the good and lost the best in the process.

And now the circle has come back around to us – what will we choose?

The problem that confronts us is that modern Christianity attempts to step around that question. It wants to settle for the good in humanity instead of the best of God – and if that is the case, then there is no question to answer and no choice to make. We simply stick with the status quo and continue doing the best we can in life.

But if we are determined to avoid the question, then we are choosing to miss out on the adventure of life in the Spirit – *and that is a trip no one should miss!*

CHAPTER 8
All In A Good Cause

Christianity is known for its many causes.

Talk about diversity, the Bread of Life has been piled so high with toppings that we can hardly see the Bread anymore.

Every kind of charity and missionary outreach, marriage enrichment and financial management programs, church building programs, leadership and ministry training, prayer ministry and inner healing proliferate our lives to name just a few. But in addition to this we have our pet subjects like creation science, end times, prosperity teaching, relationship building, Christian politics, community activities, and the list goes on, and on, and on…

Paul wasn't into it; in his own words, "For I resolved to know nothing while I was with you except Jesus Christ and him crucified". (1 Corinthians 2:2)

Why do you think that was? He certainly had an extensive resume to draw upon, and the diversity of his life experiences certainly qualified him to relate on all levels; but he chose not to go there.

Instead he limited himself to one subject alone. Listen to him speak:

I consider everything a loss because of the surpassing worth of knowing Christ Jesus my Lord / I want to know Christ and the power of His resurrection and the fellowship of His sufferings, being conformed to Him in His death / When Christ, who is your life, appears… / Then you, being rooted and grounded in love, may have power, together with all the saints, to comprehend the length and width and height and depth of His love, and to know the love of Christ that surpasses knowledge, that you may be filled with all the fullness of God…

Paul didn't have time for all the offshoots and side roads of Christianity; he was so obsessed by the wonder and extravagance of Christ that to speak of anything else would defy all logic to him. Christ filled his screen; He overwhelmed him. The living Christ filled and satisfied every crevice of his being.

> *Paul was a man possessed in the best possible way;*
> *he was possessed by an insatiable appetite for Jesus.*

Paul was so fixated by the Bread of Life that the diverse toppings of Christianity were irrelevant; the Bread satisfied him, energised him and gave him life without the addition of any other ingredient.

It's one of the things I began to ponder as I was coming to the end of my fifty-five-year sojourn into Adam's version of Christianity: Where is Christ? Who is Christ? Why don't we talk about Him like Paul did anymore? It was like we were a little bit awkward about Him, as if talking about Him would make us look fanatical or something.

Yet it's hard to discount His place among us; we named this whole thing after Him after all. Like the elephant in the room, we know He is there; but we're just not quite sure what to do with Him. So we assign Him naming rights and get on with a form of Christianity that we are more comfortable with, one that appeals better to our topping of choice.

I am convinced that the reason we don't talk about Him is that we don't know Him. We know a little bit about Him, so we talk about that; and we like some of the things He did, so we talk about that; but it's difficult to talk with any confidence about someone who hasn't been around for 2,000 years, so we don't.

In fact, it's a bit weird to talk personally about someone so distant; so we speak of Him somewhat theoretically as our founder, guide and inspiration, and then go about continuing the mission He began. The mission in all its forms then becomes that platform upon which we build our faith, and so we are known as a distribution centre of all things Christian, instead of the body of people who have the indwelling presence of the Living God.

> *You can't talk about what you don't have, so we don't.*

Instead we talk about what we do have, and passionately engage ourselves in our preferred topping, leaving the religious stuff to others who are so inclined.

But it's not too late, I waited until I was fifty-five, but at least I didn't wait until I was ninety-five. I'm sixty-five now, and the last ten years have been beyond wonderful – it's never too late.

The key is to begin talking to our Father about Jesus; asking who He was, why He came, what He accomplished in His coming, and who we are as a result. The important thing is that we begin the process of coming to terms with something so spectacular that we would dare give up who we are to have it. That's repentance, walking away from a past life to embrace a new one – so we need to get a handle on what all the fuss is about, to see if it's worth doing.

It's funny to think that Paul spoke of his one obsession – 'to know Christ' – as if that was all he ever did. But we know that he did so much more, and that the known world was changed by him in just a few short years. Yet in Paul's mind, all he was doing was 'knowing Christ'; the rest overflowed from the wonder of knowing Him.

The same is true for us, without the extraordinary joy of knowing Christ, all we are doing is scattering our toppings around; but with that knowledge we are able to feed a hungry world with the Bread of Life.

Before I began feeding on the Bread of Life, I found the Christian imperatives of witnessing and sharing the gospel a drudgery which I avoided at all costs. Now I talk about Jesus freely and spontaneously because I know Him. At last I am able to give Him away to others, because I have Him to give away. He is no longer subject matter; now He is my life companion who has made His home in me.

I'm still involved with the distribution of toppings; there are life needs all around us that deserve our attention and care, but the thing I love to do most is talk about Jesus. His love is beyond description – *but I attempt to describe it at every opportunity anyway, I just can't help myself.*

CHAPTER 9
To Know Christ

I know a lot of people, some very intimately like my wife Angela, and some others hardly at all. I know them according to the amount of time we spend together. The more we are together, the more we come to know each other through conversation, proximity and observation.

While it is good to engage in a daily dialogue with God, that is not primarily how I know Him. I know Him as His Spirit reveals to me who He is, firstly through the Bible (the written Word), and then through the Spirit (the Living Word).

I know who God is because Jesus has revealed Him to me. It's important to know God as revealed to us by Jesus and not by Adam; these two different presentations make Him appear to be two completely different Gods.

Jesus and Adam are the two defining people of human history; we are either in one or the other. In fact, on several occasions, the Bible describes the whole human race as either one man or the other man. The first Adam contained a race of beings born of the flesh; the last Adam (Jesus) contained a race of beings reborn of the Spirit. So it follows that the perceptions Adam had of God, and the perceptions Jesus has of God, will be poles apart.

> *I used to know the God that Adam knew;*
> *now I have come to know the God that Jesus knows.*

Adam knew God according to the Tree of the Knowledge of Good and Evil; he perceived God through the lens of his personal management of all the good and evil that life brings, and so the God he knew was primarily concerned with Adam's lifestyle and behaviour.

Jesus knew God according to the Tree of Life; He perceived God through the lens of God's unconditional love quite apart from His deeds and actions, and so the God He knew was unconditionally loving and good.

Jesus knew the true God, and Adam knew a God who was distorted by his choice to live a self-managed life. In other words, Adam didn't really know God at all.

It takes quite some effort, and a certain amount of courage as well, to change our knowledge of God. The paradigms of the Tree of the Knowledge of Good and Evil are so firmly established in us that it seems reckless and irresponsible to reverse out of that space, yet deep inside we know we must. There is a voice inside us that is drawing us out of fear and into restful faith.

It was by reading the Gospel of John, and then reading it over and over again, that I began to see the difference. I noticed that Jesus referred to His Father a lot, and that woven through these references was such an assurance of His Father's love and acceptance, that Jesus was able to accomplish the impossible.

I think Jesus came to earth and suffered and died for humanity because of one fundamental thing – He understood, at the deepest and most profound level, that His Father loved humanity; and He was so knit to His Father's heart that He was compelled to express it – not because of a command from His Father, but by the overwhelming love of His Father.

His Father's love was so pure, so gloriously beautiful, and so dynamically forceful that Jesus was overwhelmed by it and helplessly caught up it in – and so He leaned back into it, and against all the earthly odds, He carried Adam's family back home again.

That is the God Jesus knew.

I hadn't seen this before. I thought of the Father's love as tolerantly benevolent and divinely condescending, but I hadn't grasped the scale and extravagance of it. Neither had I grasped the unstoppable power of it.

Adam tried to contain God's love within his cause and effect world and its inherent management of good and evil, but God's love couldn't be constrained in such a small space; and it exploded free. The explosion that occurred on the cross of Christ was so all-encompassing, so blindingly illuminating, and so staggeringly destructive that Adam's world order was wiped out in one fell swoop.

The kingdom that Adam and his descendants had spent thousands of years constructing was destroyed in an instant, and the Kingdom of God once again inhabited the hearts of God's beloved people.

> **But we can't make sense of that astounding event if we remain bound up by the thinking of Adam.**

If we shrink back from changing our perception of God and His heart of love, then that phenomenal event will mean nothing more than words on a page to us. Our thinking will be stuck in time even though we have been translated into eternity.

That was me; I was stuck in Satan's propaganda. The fictitious time warp of Adam's world held me in its orbit – even though Jesus had obliterated it.

That is a tragedy of epic proportions.

To be so released from the grip of Adam's slavery to self, and so completely reabsorbed into such an inconceivable love, yet to live as if it is all just a fanciful dream, is the greatest abuse ever perpetrated against us – because it has reduced us to a mere fraction of who we really are.

It is a miscarriage of all that our loving God had in mind when He created us as the overflow of His great heart of love, and it is the very objective of Satan's spiteful agenda against God.

If we want to show honour to God and to pay recognition to His great majesty, then we must come to terms with the scale of what Christ accomplished for and in us, and embrace it as our true selves. To do less is to discredit God's character and relegate Him to the category of mere earthly idol instead of the magnificent God He really is, the God who is love.

This is the way Jesus knew His Father. He was drawn-in and held in place by His Father's great heart – and we can know God in the same way too.

CHAPTER 10

The God Who Is Love

The redefining of God's character from loving Father to stern judge has been Satan's long-term plan, a plan in which Adam unwittingly became complicit – and by default, so did we. If Satan could stop God from being true to Himself, then Satan could have rightfully claimed the throne of heaven – and so Satan presented us with a distortion of God's true character in a vain attempt to draw God into his plan out of offended retaliation, and we have lived with that distortion for the span of human history.

What is a loving God to do in the face of such an affront? Wipe out Satan by the power of His Word, burn him to a cinder, crush him to a pulp?

The only way God could deal with such a blatant assault was to treat it for what it was – the pitiful foolishness of someone who didn't really know Him. God held the line; there was never really any doubt that He would, and He enacted the most extravagant love-based solution possible. He dug deeply into the very core of His being and responded with the most extreme act of love ever seen in human history and all eternity; He sacrificed His greatest Love to express His great love.

Satan never really saw it coming; he thought he had God on the ropes and it was just a matter of time before God sunk to his level and retaliated with brute force – but God loved us back instead.

So now we believers,
those who have become partakers of that great love,
have a choice to make
– will we live as if that great love is true or not?

Will we choose it as more than just words on a page? Will we allow our existence to be completely redefined by it? I don't mean redefined in the sense that we engage ourselves more frantically in the business of distributing our toppings, but redefined in the sense that we ourselves become partakers of the great love banquet and feed on the Bread of Life.

In exactly the same way that God would not entertain Satan's game and take action outside of His loving nature, neither will He coerce or manipulate us into conforming to the truth of His love. All He can do is put His love out there, knowing its staggering capacity to bring change, and patiently let it do its work.

> ***We do well to spend some time contemplating this;***
> ***this is not the God I grew up with.***

I don't by nature know what to do with such a God. I don't know how to be a son and heir of heaven, and I don't instinctively even get what this is all about. I can easily wrap it up in religious words and platitudes, but it seems to be pulling something more than that out of me, something that is buried so deep in the core of me that I don't instinctively know what to do about it.

It is as if there is something profoundly different in the core of my being to my habitual tendency to self-manage my life, and I don't know how to bring this inner thing to the surface.

This inner me has a voice, but it's not a pushy voice; I have to make way for it to speak. And when it speaks, it tells me about another kingdom where the love of God is the all-encompassing atmosphere, a place where the goodness of God is so overwhelmingly present that fear and doubt are unknown. And it tells me that I already live in this place and can freely partake in its reality, if I will simply dial down the persistent voice of Adam.

In the same way that God will not play Satan's game, this inner voice will not play Adam's game. It does not even understand Adam's way of perceiving God; there is simply no common ground, so it puts the extravagance of God's love out there, knowing its staggering capacity to bring change, and patiently lets it do its work.

> ***This inner voice is the Spirit of God living in my spirit.***

How extraordinary it is to think that the Spirit of God lives in me and speaks words of life to me, just because I have acknowledged the work of the cross.

This is the quest and delight of the child of God – learning how to listen to the quiet voice inside.

Some people say that God doesn't speak to them, but that's not true. God speaks to us all – but He does not speak the language of Adam. In John 6:63 we read the words, "the Spirit gives life, the flesh counts for nothing." The Spirit of God does not speak in the language of the flesh.

The language of the Spirit is 'words of life' – the Spirit gives life. The language of the flesh is the opposite – 'words of death'. The Spirit will never speak words of death.

The reason many people do not hear the voice of the Spirit is that they are waiting for Him to speak Adam's words of death.

The words of life that the Spirit speaks to us are straight from the throne of heaven; He speaks to us about the unconditional love of our Father God as expressed on the cross of Christ. In John 15:26 we read that "the Spirit testifies about Jesus" – this is His language, He cannot contradict Himself, He will only express the truth which resonates throughout heaven – Jesus' blood has done its work in us, we have been made as perfect as God.

The voice of Adam expresses a different reality. "We continue to live lives punctuated by failure and sin" – it is up to us to choose which voice will inform us of the truth. We cannot take the best of each and listen to a blended message. These messages speak from opposite ends of the spectrum; there is no common ground.

To hear the voice of the Spirit, we must shut down the voice of the flesh, which feeds us a continuous newsreel of how we are doing on the stage of life on earth. This news feed is like a TV camera that watches our every move, and then plays it back to us with a journalistic commentary dubbed over – its insistent critique has the effect of defining us by our management of life.

The commentary that is broadcast by the Spirit is a completely different message. The camera is trained on Jesus instead of us, and so we are informed of the staggering scale of the perfect sacrifice of Christ at work in us, as opposed to the self-made attempts to be righteous we picked up from Adam. This critique of the work of Christ is so astonishing that it overshadows and resolves our human failings – and we become redefined by the righteousness of Christ instead of the good and evil of Adam.

Only we can choose to be righteousness-conscious instead of sin-conscious.

Only we can decide by which voice we will be defined.

Our default setting is that we want the Spirit of God to talk to us about our management of good and evil – and that is why He seems mute at times. He has nothing to say about it, and so the air is filled with silence.

Renewing our minds is all about adjusting our internal radio station settings to a new transmission frequency – a frequency that does not know the language of Adam. We don't need the transmission frequency of Adam; the Holy Spirit has a much better way of directing our lives.

CHAPTER 11

Superstition

Superstition is not a subject we often associate with Christianity, yet there are aspects of Adam's form of Christianity which are more comfortable in superstition than faith. I'm not referring to the more extreme kind of superstition associated with the black arts, but a more acceptable version based on the notion that a force links the performance of our religious ritual with God's favour and blessing.

In Australia, the Arunta aboriginal community has a ritual where the tribal sorcerer points a magical bone at his victim while muttering curses to cause the victim to sicken and die. This activity activates such fear in the victim that the curse actually produces the intended outcome. Numerous other ancient cultures engage in control of their adherents through the performance of rituals, and Christianity contains its own subtle share of the practice.

It seems that humanity has a built-in mechanism linking ritual with blessing. Like the football player who always wears the same pair of socks when on the field because they are the ones he had on when he kicked his career-defining goal, we fear that we will be subject to bad fortune if we don't engage in our particular ritual.

In becomes a sinister practice in the Christian context because it denies the most fundamental tenet of our faith, that the blood of Christ has translated us into a continual environment of God's blessing, favour and love. It implies that God's goodness cannot be counted upon unless we placate Him by offering up a sign of our commitment.

For instance, do we need to pray for God's protection when we set out on a trip, and conversely is God withholding His protection unless we pray? What if we have a car accident in spite of the fact that we prayed? Does that make the accident God's will? And if we forget to pray and have a car accident, does that make it our fault because we neglected our responsibility?

Consider the person who has been instructed their whole life that God's financial blessing is linked to tithing. What if that person gains a new revelation of the freedom of the Spirit and the unconditional love of God? Should they dare waver from their previous confidence in tithing and simply rest in their newfound union brokered by the blood of Jesus?

These are every day challenges that we face. Dare we cast our entire sense of security upon the outcomes of the cross, or do we need to add our superstitious toppings to keep God focussed? Just because the world operates this way doesn't mean the church should.

What about the case of someone choosing to take leave of a particular fellowship, they do not need to be cursed with the dire prediction, "You are opening yourself up to attack if you step out of our covering." That is no less offensive than the practice of pointing the bone.

If we believe in Jesus, then we are covered. So long as we fix our eyes on Jesus, the package deal of faith provides us with direction, safety, joy, and all of the inheritance of faith – and our participation in church life is the joyful overflow.

> **Superstition is nothing short of a fear-based regime that keeps us from the true object of our faith – resting in the assurance of our completed salvation.**

And this superstition extends into our reading of the Bible. We have become so accustomed to looking for rules, principles, formulas, and methods for staying in God's good books that we don't know how to see through all that to the real point of it all – Jesus has set us free with the expressed purpose that we would live free. Free of the fear that we might be missing something, free of the fear that our circumstances are the measure of God's love and favour, free of the fear that if we stop doing our preferred version of Christian aerobics that God will abandon us to the dogs.

I'm putting this out there in fairly graphic terms because this problem seems to have such a hold on Christians. It is a wolf in sheep's clothing that pretends to be benign, but all the while holding Christians in its insidious trap.

God doesn't play games; He doesn't command us to learn His dance so that we can stay in step with Him. He brings us back to His kingdom and gives us His Spirit, and then He sets us free to live large in His love – *anything less than that is religious manipulation based on fear.*

In this day and age, we have a unique set of superstitions that we carry around in our bag of tricks. Loud prayer, continual prayer chains, and demonstrative expressions in praise and worship are all part of the dance steps we have learned. And at the other end of the spectrum, loud and desperate repentance, searching out hidden sins to confess, wallowing in our unrighteousness – all the actions of a person stuck in the grip of Adam's superstitious perspective of God.

We don't need to get God's attention; it is already the very atmosphere of our existence. And we don't need to pave the way into God's presence with overt activities when His presence is already the defining fact of our lives.

CHAPTER 12

Supernatural

The flip side to superstition is the supernatural. We are supernatural beings whether we like it or not; we were made supernatural (above nature) when we received the divine, eternal life of Jesus. Walking it out requires a completely different headspace to the one that is used to walk in Adam's superstition. Walking in superstition fits neatly into Adam's headspace, but to walk in the supernatural, we need to embrace the mind of Christ.

The difference between these two ways of thinking is that the mind of Christ always looks to the events of the past – the death and resurrection of Jesus. These events position the renewed mind into a state of readiness and expectation. The work is done; all that remains is for us to walk in it. The activities of Jesus have already crafted the secure environment of the future.

The mind of Adam on the other hand always looks to the future; it anticipates an outcome based on its application of some as yet unsatisfied religious ritual or spiritual activity. The mind of Adam is always in a state of hope and apprehension based on the satisfactory completion of the activities necessary to engage God in the affairs of humankind.

The mind of Adam is continually adding to and rearranging the toppings in the hope that just the right combination will move the hand and will of God.

Self-effort is the posture of the mind of Adam.

The mind of Christ is already so connected to the hand and will of God by virtue of the completed work of Christ, that it simply rests there. There is no more to be done because the Bread of Life is already the overflow of God's heart.

Resting is the posture of the mind of Christ.

The supernatural expression of God on the cross of Christ is the doorway through which we walk to activate the supernatural in our own lives. We engage in the supernatural *as* Christ, He is our new identity. Just like Jesus we live in two realms simultaneously, the realm of the Spirit and the realm of nature, and so we are as comfortable being supernatural as we are being natural.

This is not simply about obtaining impossible outcomes like healings and miracles; it is about seeing our whole life as a continually supernatural existence; everything about our life now has the supernatural touch of God upon it.

With every issue we face, we are presented afresh with the opportunity to respond supernaturally, and we do so by resting in the completed work of Christ. From the smallest of life's issues to the most challenging, all are hidden in our overarching supernatural life.

The subject of the supernatural is important to all believers because, one way or the other, we all desire for it to operate in our lives – and that desire is not limited to the Pentecostals among us who lean towards the operation of the spiritual gifts. The more conservative among us who lean towards prayer and piety also harbour such a desire. Wherever we are on the spectrum of spiritual persuasion, one end or the other or somewhere in between, there is a need to somehow engage God in our lives and the issues we face.

So the subject of the supernatural is not simply the stomping ground of left-leaning fringe groups and irrelevant to all the rest; it is implicit upon all of us because God is inherently above and beyond the constraints of nature. He is supernatural. Whether we like it or not, if we want God's hand upon our lives, we are engaging in the supernatural.

Adam left us with a seriously flawed system for engaging in the supernatural.

This flaw is based on one all-encompassing premise, that there is something we must do (whether outwardly demonstrative or more quietly expressed) that releases God's goodness, favour and blessing into our lives. Such thinking puts us into the role of 'catalyst'; we become the agent for change much like yeast is the agent for change when baking bread. If there is no catalyst, then the process of receiving blessing and favour is unable to be completed because of the missing ingredient – our engagement.

In contrast, if we rest in the nature of the bread to sustain and nourish, independently of whether it has been fluffed up by our yeast, then our participation is no more than restful confidence.

The pizza base is a great illustration. As a classic flatbread, it performs its function without the addition of any catalyst. Adam left us uncertain and insecure in regard to this restful confidence. We are more likely to frantically work the yeast into the mix rather than leaning back into the invisible heart and nature of God. Adam has pumped us up with the human response, instead of simply trusting in our union with our Heavenly Father.

This may seem like hair splitting to some who believe it doesn't really matter how we go about our engagement with God, as long as we are engaged. And I agree; how we go about the expression of our Christianity is not the point – we are free to conduct ourselves in our own unique way.

The point is not how we conduct ourselves, but how we perceive the work of Christ. In that regard, our engagement with God is the expression of how we understand Jesus and His life, death and resurrection, and that is of paramount importance.

This is where the 'doing' nature of Adam is so sinister; it adds an intermediate component to the expression of God's nature, which effectively disengages it. God's love, favour, blessing and goodness is unconditionally and freely given. It is a river of life flowing from His heart to ours – if we add a human element to that flow, then we effectively dam up the flow behind the satisfactory performance of that human element. No matter how spiritual our input may seem, it is not God's requirement to release His flow of life – He simply calls us to rest in His love.

All of this can leave us a little bit lost as we flounder around trying to figure out who we are if God doesn't require us to engage in our familiar spiritual activities. And that is just where God wants us. The lostness of bringing nothing to Him but confidence in His love positions us to engage with Him in the way that humanity was originally designed – being carried by His Spirit.

By disengaging our dependence on human rituals, we engage supernatural life.

Just a disclaimer for those who think I am advocating a cheap and irresponsible lifestyle: To boldly stand before God clothed only in the virtue of Christ is the most courageous thing we can do. It stands head and shoulders above any activity we might perform in the hope of leavening the bread, *which requires no such leavening.* It is a declaration that Christ is enough, and that we have chosen to take up His challenge to feed on Him alone.

CHAPTER 13
Feeding On Christ

If ever Jesus made a confrontational statement, it was the time when He told His followers that unless they ate His body and drank His blood, they would have no part in Him… and they left in droves. Jesus wasn't simply providing a useful illustration for us to read during Holy Communion; this was far more graphic and pointed than that.

Jesus had decided that the time was right to draw a line in the sand, and that it was necessary for His disciples to be confronted by that line, so they would step over it and partake in the fullness of His life once and for all.

Did Jesus make a mistake by being so confrontational? Perhaps He should have been a little more accommodating (and a bit less macabre in His use of metaphor), but He didn't, He put the truth out there in such a dramatic way that it was impossible to sit on the fence.

He did it because there is no life in sitting on the fence, in being a spectator – so it is better that we are either hot or cold, full on or full off. Jesus didn't do this because He was intent on galvanizing them into action or preparing them for a life of demanding service. He did it because it is impossible to partake in the life that He came to give unless we believe in it – to the extent that we completely lose ourselves in it.

The pizza topping mentality which pervades much of Christianity is not the same as losing ourselves in His sacrifice; we might be just participating in His club.

Think about it; can you imagine yourself eating a chunk of Jesus' flesh or tipping a pint of His blood down your throat – it defies every rational thought and sensibility we hold dear. Yet that is the way Jesus chose to describe our participation in His life; it is a deliberate description that shakes us free of the lesser alternative of merely following His teachings and compels us to embrace the most confronting claim possible – that we feed on His being.

He was actually describing the true life of faith – not the faith in which we engage by pumping up our own spiritual aerobics, but a faith which examines the sensationally scandalous and exorbitant claims of Jesus, and against all rational judgement chooses to be completely redefined by them.

We are not flesh-eating people, and neither are we given to being defined by scandal. But the fact remains that if the claims of Jesus are not disturbing our sense of order, then we are missing something.

The normalising of Christianity has turned us into followers instead of feeders (to use Jesus' own words), but how exactly do we feed on Christ?

Okay, enough with the cannibalistic imagery; let's get down to the hard facts of the matter.

To eat Jesus' flesh and drink His blood is to partake in the death and resurrection of Jesus at a much deeper level than simply participating in church life, being good, and generally involving ourselves in the great big thing called Christianity. It is to embrace the Spirit of Jesus in such a way that we no longer live apart from Him; we have no life apart from the life that is saturated in the reality of His cross.

We continue to live and laugh, to love, to play and work – we do all the things that normal inhabitants of the planet do, but now we engage in these activities as strangers and aliens, looking at life on earth through the eyes of those who are also seated with Christ in glory.

> *We are a strange new breed who are completely here,*
> *yet not here.*

The earth cannot hold us because we are no longer of the earth; we have feasted on the life of Jesus and been changed, magnificently transformed on the inside into replicas of Christ. All this because we choose not to be offended by the scandal of the cross of Christ.

So don't be put off by all this because it sounds a bit spooky; it isn't. Living supernaturally is the most natural way for us to live. It just takes some time to get used to it. It takes a little while for us to get reaccustomed to the way God made us before Adam's defection. Be patient; it will become clearer with each passing day.

That was the experience of the disciples. They started out wondering what it was all about – and eventually became so clear in their understanding of what Jesus had accomplished that such statements as "I have been crucified with Christ" became their normal daily reality.

And we are the same, the full reality of what we are in may still be a little unclear – but it will come as we fix our eyes on Jesus the author and perfector of our faith.

The transition from our identity as toppings to our identity as 'hidden in the bread' is a completely new headspace. The diversity of giftings, ministry and expression is all swallowed up in the one overarching fact of our identity in Christ – what we do is no longer the point of it all, but who we have become.

This new identity won't work, it won't settle in to us, unless we come to terms with Jesus' teaching about feeding on Him. In other words, these two are intrinsically linked; we cannot come to terms with 'who we have become' unless we also choose to 'feed on Christ'.

For much of my Christian life I attempted to apprehend my identity in Christ by discovering it through the numerous promises and statements made in the Bible. I thought I could embrace my new identity by changing my language and replacing my old narrative with a new and better one, but it didn't work. Eventually my old narrative overtook me again, and I found that my identity was back where it had always been – bogged down in my 'doing' thinking.

I had inadvertently been using Adam's approach to lay hold of Christ's work.

Adam thought he could train himself to be spiritual, that all it took was a bit of determination and application sprinkled with a good confession, and out would pop a new spiritual man – and I was stuck in his thinking. Eventually I had to admit that I was no better off than Adam in the self-made spirituality game.

To escape this exhausting cycle of self-improvement, I had to stop being me.

This 'ceasing to be me' could not be grasped through my old practices. It was not able to be obtained through a process or a program. Nothing was available in all the diversity of the Christian culture that could do what I needed.

I needed to stop being a topping, and for that I had to die.

I could not retain my status as a topping and simply change my rhetoric to that of the bread; I needed to actually cease being one to embrace the other.

My only option was to truly be crucified with Christ.

CHAPTER 14

Crucified With Christ

Paul's statement about being crucified with Christ is a bit like Jesus' statement about eating His body and drinking His blood – it is confrontational and a little off-putting. But it doesn't have to be that way; this is not a thing to shy away from because it is extreme or unsettling. This is actually the way we were designed when we were first conceived in the mind of God; it is God's 'normal' for us.

Adam raised up a being which is so removed from our true restful design that it barely resembles the original, and we have become so familiar with this model that we can't imagine living any other way.

Jesus has remade us according to God's original 'normal'. The normal that Adam inserted into our nature has been completely made redundant, so it is both logical and beneficial for us to re-embrace the nature of Christ and ease back into His love and goodness.

What Jesus accomplished on the cross was dramatically more far reaching than simply the payment of a punishment due us as a result of our sins; it was a complete destruction of the person who lived within the nature that is controlled by sin.

> ***Jesus did more than pay the price;***
> ***He deconstructed the being that Adam made us into.***

Like Paul, we no longer live – yet we remain attached to the model that Adam designed for us because we haven't grasped the lavish work of the cross. We live as if the work of Adam is greater than the work of Christ.

And the hallmark of the work of Adam is that we are more defined by our toppings (the things we do), than the bread (our existence in Christ).

This ends with our crucifixion with Christ.

The perpetuation of a life that is defined by 'our doing' is now inconceivable. Why would we wish to be defined by the meagre nature of Adam when the extravagant nature of Jesus is available to us?

And so the journey of discovery begins – the journey into the true us.

"I have been crucified with Christ and I no longer live, but Christ lives in me. The life I now live in the body, I live by faith in the Son of God, who loved me and gave himself for me". (Galatians 2:20)

The idea that "I no longer live, but Christ lives in me" is a bit difficult to process. We can do it lip service, and in broad terms give it our nod of approval; but to actually live that way can be somewhat elusive.

So it's important to have a fresh look at this, it's important to gain a perspective which is not constrained or tainted by the thinking of the past – we must see this as God does.

Why is it so important to God that we be crucified? What is it about us that must be done away with to enable us to stand in His presence? And finally, and above all; what is it about the nature of Adam, which is so opposite to my true design, that the most loving thing God can do for me is kill me?

When Jesus died on the cross, He carried in Himself the entire family of Adam. Every one of us that was contaminated by the spiritual sickness of Adam was subjected to the greatest genocide ever seen in human history. The human race was wiped from the face of the earth as surely as it was in the great flood of Noah. None survived; it was catastrophic.

No human being had the capacity to willingly participate in this event. We were all beyond participation, so debilitated and weakened by the epidemic of Adam's making that we could only stand by and watch it happen in stupefied unbelief. Yet the power of the sacrifice of Christ was so potent that it morphed the whole lot of us into it, and we disappeared into the vortex of His suffering.

Christ saved us from ourselves, and we had no say in the matter.

If that is the case, why then is the whole human race not saved?

We are all saved – but we must believe it, to receive it. The work of the cross is as complete and real for the wicked and cruel, as it is for the rest of us – and now we can partake or not; it is up to us. "God so loved the *world* that he sent His only Son, that whoever *believes* in Him will be saved" (John 3:16). God sent Jesus to save the world, and we can participate in that salvation by believing in it.

The remarkable thing about this salvation is not only the staggering scale of its solution for humanity, but also the meagre few who actually want it – such is the hold that the legacy of Adam has on us. And further to that, it is remarkable that so many people around the world are drawn to belief in the message of the gospel, but lack the conviction to be *completely* redefined by the totality of it. The halls of Christendom are largely populated by people who don't know what they have, and remain living as if they are still alive in Adam when they have actually been crucified with Christ.

We remain alive in Adam by up-valuing all the things we do here on earth and down-valuing what Christ did in giving us His divine life on the cross. What we do on this earth has value; we cannot deny that a life of service and decency is of worth. However, it is comparatively worthless when placed alongside the spectacular gift of life that we received from Jesus.

And so we live in a type of deformity which is actually not true of us that, like Adam, we are the sum of our management of good and evil – when in reality that self-defining fact was crucified with Christ, and we were reborn anew of God.

To be crucified with Christ is to walk away from self.

Not selfishness, but self-sufficiency – selfishness and self-sufficiency are two completely different matters.

Selfishness is generally the outcome of a far more deep-seated problem, self-sufficiency – but self-sufficiency is actually our real problem because it competes with Christ for our identity. Self-sufficiency poses as a harmless and even virtuous characteristic, but it is far from harmless when it keeps alive that which Christ has crucified.

Self-sufficiency defines the nature of Adam which stood between us and God. It is so opposite of our true design, and so deeply entrenched in our being, that the most loving thing God could do for us was kill us. He did this because the very best way for us to live is to restfully walk in the way He planned at the start, completely and selflessly dependent upon His Spirit for our life.

To be crucified with Christ is to embrace this new way.

The Scriptures often record Jesus' exhortation to His followers to unburden themselves onto Him. "Come to me all who labour and are heavy laden and I will give you rest". He is calling us to abandon our self-sufficiency and lean on His capacity to be our sufficiency and carry us through life.

This is our true design.

It is more than a reprieve from the battles of life before we re-enter the fray and slug it out all over again; it is the way God intended us to live for every minute of every day of our time on earth.

The self-sufficiency of Adam competes with God for our identity so powerfully that God had to kill it. They were incompatible and could not successfully inhabit us together – one had to go. This is why Jesus came, that we might be freed to choose once again to rest in His sufficiency and love.

When we make that choice, we no longer live – but Christ lives in us.

If we don't make that choice, then we are opting by default to live in opposition to that truth – the truth that Jesus has destroyed the old to make way for the new.

CHAPTER 15

The Pizza Of Self

We Christians often find our identity in what we do, and why not? We do a lot of good things. Some among us are very secure in this space; they feel they are doing a pretty good job... *but is it good enough*? Others are quite insecure; they are worried that they are never doing well enough. So constructing our security, and being defined by the good we do, has problems no matter where we sit on the scale.

The pizza topping mentality that pervades much of Christianity only contributes to the problem. It provides us with so many options by which to be defined that, in some way or other, it is able to scoop us all up into its false sense of security.

Most pizza toppings are good, so it's not a question of the comparative worth of our area of ministry, passion, service or interest. It is about whether the things that we have constructed around us to provide us with our sense of place in the great big Christian machine are actually able to do it.

Some people have a unique passion, others a talent or gifting, and still others an area of humble service; and these are all good in their way. But when they eclipse the wonder of our love union with Christ, they end up diminishing the greatest thing of all, and that's when it's time to take a few steps back and have a fresh look at things all over again.

We have a unique capacity within all of us to mismanage the area of identity; we may think that our identity is wrapped up in one thing, but the way we live shows that it is actually founded on something entirely different. It's not that we are deliberately lying to ourselves or others; it's more that we haven't understood that the thing to which we gravitate and speak of the most is actually what defines us.

So it's quite possible for us to mentally and theological embrace the truth about Jesus, but then live our lives on the basis of a completely different truth.

For instance, I know a young woman who is often heard to declare aloud during worship that "Jesus is everything", yet when I recently met her friends, they didn't know she was a Christian – so, clearly, Jesus wasn't everything. To be defined by the truth of who Christ is means that we elevate that truth to the greatest reality in our lives… *and our friends won't be able to miss it.*

This is not an analysis of our witnessing record; it is a reality check that sometimes we think we are defined by a certain thing, when in fact we aren't at all. Sometimes we think we are defined as people who trust in Jesus, when in fact all we do is talk about trust while living our lives in fear.

To be defined by Christ is more than simply repeating the words.

Others among us are much more realistic; they know in their hearts that they are not living as people who are truly defined by the sacrifice of Jesus, so they never claim to be, and settle for being openly defined by their preferred topping instead.

More often than not, though, we don't define ourselves by the sacrifice of Jesus because we don't understand that such an option is truly available to us. So we file it away in our theological folder to be opened on Sunday and settle instead for being good people who share their toppings around.

The tragedy is that such an option is actually available to all of us right now.

For example, I am a building designer and project manager by trade. I have been involved in building design and construction in some way for the whole of my work life; I am very comfortable and confident in that space. At times I have also expressed that ability in the church context through involvement in various church or mission-related building programs. Although many people recognise that capacity in me because it is a very visible activity within the context of the church community, it is greatly overshadowed by the invisible transformation that Christ wrought in me on the cross. So it vies for my identity as a Christian. If someone asks me to tell them about myself, I can either respond in the context of my earthly identity or my heavenly one. I may be more likely to respond on the basis of the visible realm, yet my heavenly identity is the true me in a far greater way than my earthly identity – *in fact, it is the real me.*

I am also involved in many 'spiritual' activities like writing, preaching and leading worship, but as spiritual as these activities may be, they still remain the earthly expression of my revelation of Christ, and do not compare with Christ's expression of love on the cross.

The importance or need for our area of ministry or service in the body of Christ does not elevate it to parity with the shed blood of Jesus, so it is vital that we come to terms with the Bread of Life and discover how to re-elevate it back to its life-defining place in us. Otherwise, we perpetuate Adam's folly and are more defined by our acts of goodness than the extravagant love of God.

The only problem that comes with re-elevating our identity as the objects of God's love to the highest status is that whatever is presently defining us must be downgraded – and that is something most of us don't want to do… *particularly if we are very good.*

Remember when Jesus said, "the first will be last and the last will be first"? I believe He was referring to this very issue. Many of those who are very good, talented and self-confident among us will be last, because they have chosen to overvalue their personal qualities above the value of the freely given and unconditional love of God.

> **It's sobering to think that the good in us
> can hold us back from the best in God.**

Who am I? I am not the sum of my earthly abilities and values, my possessions and appearance; I am the dearest possession of the Living God of Heaven and earth.

CHAPTER 16

The Popular Mix

Yet another seemingly benign addition to our faith in Jesus is to accompany it with a broader philosophy of life. When that happens, Jesus becomes a silent partner within our greater sphere of ideology and values.

An obvious example is the trend today to mix prosperity teaching with Christ. Jesus doesn't have a problem with our prosperity, but it isn't why He came. Earthly prosperity may well make our lives more comfortable, but Jesus didn't suffer and die the cruellest death that we might have more money in our pockets; He did it to reconnect us to His Father.

It is when the lines are blurred between our earthly lifestyle and the precious blood of Jesus that Christianity is at its most sinister.

We may indeed be able to employ many good biblical principles to improve our lives, and numerous practices and programs to bring out the best in us; but don't confuse these for the spiritual transformation that Jesus accomplished in His death and resurrection. Mixing our diverse earthly objectives with spiritual life is not the point of Christianity.

Numerous programs are on offer in the Christian culture which are helpful in showing us how to live wiser and better, but we should never confuse this self-improvement in the natural realm with the divine spiritual life Jesus came to give us lest the point of our connection with Christ be reduced to 'enabler of our better physical life management', instead of 'provider of the life that flows out of the heart of God'.

Now comes the hard part – getting to the specifics.

I said at the beginning of this book that the church has, in effect, become a reflection of humanity – and the diversity, opinions, causes and purposes observed in the wider world have become reflected in the church too, with the result that it's difficult to nail down what the word 'Christian' means anymore.

This is especially so with respect to the mixing of faith in Jesus with our broader lifestyle ideology.

It is a problem because, in many cases, our broader lifestyle ideologies actually work. Good eating habits and exercise, sensible money management, loving relationship practices – are all lifestyle choices that work and should be encouraged in the Christian community.

But we must be careful not to mix them in as part of the overall package of salvation, because that would render the blood of Jesus to a mere supporting role.

The word 'Christian' is not a lifestyle thing.

Sure, it will have lifestyle spinoffs, but these outcomes cannot be compared in value to the stellar accomplishment of Jesus when He rescued us from the grip of Satan and set us back into His Father's arms. If we well-meaning Christians cannot see the scale of the work that Jesus accomplished, then we are likely to be distracted by the more visible lifestyle improvements that we accomplish through our programs and life principles.

But in so doing we diminish Christ.

It is the diminishing of Christ which is the greatest concern; anything (no matter how good) that swings our gaze away from Him is problematic. For many people this will seem like an extreme position to take, and one that is unnecessarily firm. If the physically well-being of people were all that is at stake, I would agree; but we fall into the same snare as Adam when we perceive our existence primarily on the basis of our handling of good and evil – when in reality our true design is based on something radically greater.

We were created to be held by God's love.

Leaving that subject to one side for now, a tendency to embrace philosophies which are patently not Christian has also recently appeared in Christianity. In particular, I am speaking of the notion of assigning to God the New Age status of the energy of the universe, or perhaps a spirit life to which we are all mystically connected.

These philosophies that depersonalize God into a spiritual energy rather than a person who loves us may seem to be the logical thought progression of a modern society – but once again, to diminish Christ in any way is no Christianity at all.

Christianity is not an evolving faith; we do ourselves no benefit and God no honour when we move with the times and mix in the world's perceptions. Christianity cannot be modernised. It is based on the most ancient ideal ever conceived – the unconditional love of God – and we cannot reshape it to fit in with the mood of society.

Sure, it may enhance the world's perceptions of us, but fitting in is not the point of Christianity – we are in such stark contrast to the rest of the world that we bear no comparison at all. In fact, we shouldn't even be trying to match the world, or compete with its values and ways of expressing itself – there is no competition. Let the world be the best at what it values, and we will have Christ and Him crucified.

Such things as church government, church music, social media, and church programs have all been revamped in our attempts to keep up with the world – but we are not of this world, so why all the effort? Our message is not that we can be more excellent than the world at their own game; our message is that we are empty without Christ.

The message of excellence which is so often bandied around in Christian circles is irrelevant if we have not been profoundly moved and redefined by the excellence of Christ.

So whether it be lifestyle-based improvement programs, embracing new age philosophies, or competing with the world on their own terms, none of it can stand alongside the surpassing greatness of knowing Christ Jesus our Lord.

*Nothing can have our identity but Christ,
no matter how impressive or compelling it is.*

CHAPTER 17

Knowing Christ

Paul spent a lot of time in his letters explaining to the churches what Christianity isn't, then he went on to express in lavish terms the surpassing greatness and wonder he found in knowing Christ. I want to take his lead now and swing our focus onto something so extraordinary that our preoccupation with earthly things is brought into its proper perspective.

For most of my life, I thought the term 'knowing Christ' fitted somewhere between hopeful speculation and impressive Christian language – in other words, I thought it was more of a good ideal that we talked about rather than an actual reality. It seemed to be an idea that we ran in parallel with our human relationships, and that knowing God was like all our other relationships which hinged on spending quality time together.

Paul was able to provide us with such graphic descriptions of what it means to know Christ because he had seen something most of us don't see, and it took his perceptions of this relationship way beyond the human comparisons we usually use to understand it. Paul had been struck blind by the radiant presence of Jesus and asked, "Who are You, Lord?" He had been to the third heaven and seen things he could not even talk about. Paul had some dramatic first-hand material to work with.

I don't have a resume like Paul's, but I know some things all the same.

We all do. It's just a matter of shuffling what we know into a different order. Paul shuffled his perceptions about God too. In his case, it took some dramatic events to get him there; but the stark reality of his union with Christ eventually found its way to the top of the pile, and he was transformed for life.

This vista of the magnificence of Christ consumed Paul, and it became his obsession once the reality of it reached the surface. Nothing else came close to it; he was a willing captive to this one ecstatic truth – and from this truth he discovered that he 'knew Christ'.

Listen to what he says in Philippians 3:8: "What is more, I consider everything a loss because of the surpassing worth of knowing Christ Jesus my Lord, for whose sake I have lost all things. I consider them garbage, that I may gain Christ".

Paul didn't care about his impressive resume. It didn't register in his thinking that he had done and experienced more extraordinary things than possibly anyone else on the planet; all of that paled into insignificance compared to the glorious union he shared with Jesus – a union which energized him to live an impossible life.

We automatically think that Paul must have spent a lot of time in quiet meditation and prayer to maintain that level of intimacy, and that he must have habitually stepped out of the demands of life and into his place of quality God-time to recharge his spiritual batteries for the next demanding task he faced. Maybe he did these things. Who knows? But it seems to me there was something much greater at play which strengthened and propelled Paul to move forward.

His relationship with God was not dependent upon input from both parties to keep it vibrant and alive – like we would think of a mutual relationship today. It was more akin to the relationship that Adam had with God before he struck out on his own; it was maintained in its vibrancy and life because it flowed out of the heart of God. Adam's only part was to revel in it.

And that's what Paul did; he revelled in the heart of God.

It was a different kind of relationship to the ones we are accustomed to; it flowed spontaneously and freely out of the nature of God and required no reciprocal input but to receive it as the lavish gift it was.

Once Paul had shuffled his perceptions of God back to the original settings that Adam first knew, a whole new way of being 'in relationship' became apparent. Paul began to know God in a way that had been lost to humanity since Adam's Independence Day. He knew God according to God's heart, not man's religious protocols.

**Paul ceased knowing God Adam's way
and began knowing God Jesus' way.**

This knowledge of God is best encapsulated in the term 'rest', as so beautifully expressed in Hebrews 4:10, "For anyone who enters God's rest also rests from their works, just as God did from his". We rest from any and all of Adam's relationship maintenance obligations and simply lean in to the heart of God.

It takes quite some shuffling to get the 'rest' card to the top of the pile; we instinctively keep moving it to the lower slots because it doesn't make sense, we are so unfamiliar with the true heart of God.

So we cycle the 'rest' card around and around, giving it top deck status occasionally when things are going well, but quickly reshuffling it to the lower order when things get a bit bumpy to make way for activities in which we feel safer in the hope that they might reinforce our God connections.

But Jesus cannot be contained in any activity that is not anchored in our rest in the unconditional love of His Father. If He could be so contained, He would be just a man like us. The extravagance of His love for humanity is so great that it renders all of our inbuilt correctness defunct; He calls us to rest in His love without the support of any reciprocal action – because His love is able to do both.

The love of God is so all-encompassing that it not only provides God's part, but it also provides our part. God does both, as Paul explains so well in Ephesians 35:25-27. God loves us so much that He cleansed us and made us holy, and presents us back to Himself… He does it all.

Our only role is to believe that His love could be that good and rest in it.

And when we finally get that, everything changes. We begin to live in a love so immeasurable that our corresponding response is replaced by the glorious restfulness of our true design.

This is what Paul discovered. His initial question – "Who are you, Lord?" – was ultimately answered in a way that was more extravagant than Paul could have hoped for or imagined: I am the one who loves you beyond your wildest dreams, and my love will never leave you or forsake you.

Once Paul had his question answered and had shuffled that answer to the top, a completely new way to live opened up to him. He became so energized by that love that he began to live a life fuelled by God's love-motivated power... and he achieved the impossible.

And it was all because Paul shifted the focus away from himself and his self-effort, and onto the spectacular love-energy of Christ.

Paul knew God in God's way. It was exactly the same way Adam did when he first opened his eyes as the object of God's immense love. Adam knew that by resting in God's nature of unrestricted love, his own nature as the object of that love could be restfully yet dynamically expressed into the natural realm (how sad he didn't remain there).

Jesus did it too (in the same way that Adam did in the very beginning). He rested in His Father's love, and His Father's divine energy flowed through all that He did. Paul picked up on it turned the known world upside down as a result. Others, like the apostles John and Peter, were similarly transformed by this love revelation and modelled a new way to restfully live (as believers carried through life by God's love) because of it.

And now we can live that way too.

CHAPTER 18

Resting In Love

Some things disappeared from sight when Adam chose to independently construct his identity from his management of good and evil, instead of leaning into his love union with God for it. A great many casualties resulted from this choice, but perhaps the greatest casualty of all was the loss of our instinctive ability to hide ourselves in the security of God's love.

Even now, with the teaching of God's grace proliferating the Christian airwaves, we do not find it easy to rest in Him. We have made the transition from law to grace, which has lifted a great load from our shoulders, but we haven't proceeded all the way to the intended end goal.

Grace is nothing more and nothing less than a doorway. It is not the gospel; it is the price of receiving the gospel – so it is important to progress all the way into what that grace purchased for us. The grace of God (expressed through the freely given sacrifice of Christ) has purchased for us full and free access to the heart of God, which was God's initiative – now we must walk through the doorway of grace and into the freedom of resting in God's love, which is our part.

It is important that terms like 'the gospel of grace' do not confuse us, because the only gospel is the gospel of Jesus Christ. We enter into Christ through the doorway of grace. It's not enough to have simply resolved the tension that comes with the burden of the law, and embraced the ease that comes with the lightness of grace; if so, we are likely to simply turn our frown into a smile and embrace a happier form of Christianity – but not really know who we are, or why.

The point of grace is that we re-discover our restful love union with God; if all we have discovered is a happier Christian disposition, then we have barely scratched the surface at all.

Jesus didn't come to make us feel better; He came to kill us so that we can be reborn as people who are instinctively able to hide ourselves in the security of God's love… there is a big difference.

The first option holds us in the natural realm; it simply resolves the oppression that comes from the law and our emotional tension that accompanies it. The second translates us to the spiritual realm where there is no law or tension; it is an entirely new environment.

This new spiritual environment is primarily characterised by the unconditional love of God, and we as citizens of this kingdom are designed to be nurtured, energized and held in place by that love.

Now that we understand that this is God's intention, the next step is to learn to live in it.

To live in this state of blissful rest, we need to reactivate an instinct that was lost when Adam and Eve took leave of the environment of God's unconditional love. In other words, we need to re-learn how to be truly human.

The innate ability to be carried through life by the love of God (our true and original design) is hidden deep down inside all of us; it was given back to the human race when Jesus carried in Himself the entire family of Adam and crucified our spiritual depravity on His cross. He remade us with all of the instincts we need to rest in the unconditional love of God – and now that is the true us.

Yet, like Adam, we remain people with a choice.

> *So the issue for us is not whether we qualify for God's love,*
> *but whether we choose to rest in it.*

This is the great casualty I mentioned earlier – that we can have so much, yet continue to live in such uncertainty because we are not deeply convinced that the unconditional love of God really is our new environment and identity.

I won't spend any more time examining this dilemma; it is what it is. I can't convince anyone to hide themselves in the security of the cross of Christ; each of us must square up to it in our own way and determine if it was enough for us. As I said, we remain people with a choice.

So let's turn our attention to this new person that Jesus created on the cross.

What was it that was accomplished in the death and resurrection of Christ which makes us so different to our previous condition?

In Adam, we went through life with a spiritual disability; we could not see the unconditional love of God. In Jesus, we have been made whole; the disability of our spiritual blindness has been healed, and we are once again able to see the true nature of God.

The ability to see God's unconditional love was obscured by Adam's determination to self-generate his own righteousness; Adam effectively made the unconditional heart of God conditional upon his own performance in the theatre of human life.

Jesus has given us back our original design, and now we can live the way we were meant to – as people who are nurtured, energized and held in place by that love.

This is where everything changes; we can now respond to life according to our new sight.

Imagine a situation where the circumstances of life are pressing in. We can now look at that circumstance through the filter of God's unconditional love, and that filter changes the nature of the circumstance. This is not simply a religious exercise or mind game that we employ; it is the most basic fact of our new environment. We do not make it so; the blood of Jesus does.

The filter of God's love changes everything because it exposes our entire existence to a higher and better truth than the one Adam handed on to us – 'that we are safe in God'. Adam told us we weren't safe in God unless we satisfied Him by our pleasing behaviour; Jesus tells us we are safe in God because of His unconditional love.

If we are safe in God, *then we are safe in God* – everything in our lives, every circumstance and issue is held, with us, in that safe place. We do not fear anymore because the circumstances and issues of life are so overshadowed by the extravagance of God's love, that all we do is rest in His ability to care for us.

If you cannot see the extravagance of His love, then don't attempt to conjure it up by some religious activity. It is not activated by what we do, but by what we can see that Christ did.

If we could pop our heads through the clouds of our physical existence and see for a minute into the environment of heaven, we would see a love so astounding and all-encompassing that we would abandon all our fears to it in a heartbeat, so we must relocate our thinking into that new environment.

Heaven is our home, and God is our source of life. We are safe there. No, we are more than safe – we are transformed into His nature, and now we can truly rest in that fact.

CHAPTER 19
God's Toppings

Considering what we now know about God's unconditional love, the pizza which is 'me' takes on a whole new composition, and we find that the ingredients which seemed so important in Adam's assemblage begin to lose their significance. It had previously seemed so right and obvious that we should top the Bread of Life with our many and diverse activities, causes and programs; but now that the astonishing scale and wonder of God's love has come into focus, we find ourselves wondering if it's all really as important as we first thought.

Our new appreciation for the all-surpassing loving nature of God is so arresting that we find ourselves stunned by it and rendered inert for a time while we allow it to really settle upon us. To our great surprise, we find that we have become so enraptured by the immeasurable love of Jesus that we almost daren't breathe for fear of disturbing its heavenly purity with our earthly fidgeting.

Spare a thought for Peter when Jesus was suddenly transfigured before His eyes, and Moses and Elijah appeared and talked with Jesus. All Peter could think of was building a few tents for them to sit in. The spectacle which is the love of God can leave us equally bewildered – we want to do something, but we don't know what, and so we scratch together some earthly toppings and ask Jesus to hop in... *if He wouldn't mind.*

> *But He won't climb into our earthly constructs;*
> *He is more at home in His Father's love.*

Peter had never seen Jesus like that before, the glory of Jesus' transfiguration rendered Peter's normal response quite silly in the scheme of things. It was such an earthly attempt to contain something which was so dramatically unearthly.

A different Peter emerged when the full impact of Jesus' death and resurrection began to take hold; he chose to step into the work of Christ, rather than asking Jesus to step into his earthy activities – and a whole different outcome unfolded as a result.

It's like that with so much of our Christianity, the old makes way for the new, and nowhere more obviously than in our expression of the indwelling of God's Spirit. Our values shift so significantly as we behold the spectacle which is the glorious radiance of God's love expressed upon the cross that our old attachments to programs and causes fall away to make way for the dynamic life of the Spirit.

Like Paul, we begin to consider everything rubbish compared to the surpassing value of knowing Christ. It's not that our earthly programs and causes are not of benefit or value, but that they seem to diminish before our eyes as the potential of life in the Spirit gains traction in us.

We didn't expect it to be like this; like Peter we find ourselves surprised and a little unsettled that there is more going on here than we first thought. Also, we don't know what to do about all the toppings we have arranged so carefully onto the Bread of Life… *what to do?*

> *That is not the question though.*
> *Instead, we should be asking, "Who to be?"*

Please don't feel that I am trying to destabilize your present involvements; that is not what this is about. Rather, it is about discovering afresh the life behind all that we do and allowing the work of the cross to energize every endeavour in the best possible way. If we are willing to elevate the identity we have as the objects of God's unconditional love to be our life-defining truth, then all that we put our hands to will be empowered by the dynamic energy of the Spirit of God.

> *This is not about the tasks we feel fit us best;*
> *it is about the identity that fits us best.*

It's about making us specific again.

My opening line in this book was, "To be Christian has become a very unspecific thing" – Jesus came to reverse our diversity. He came to give us back the one thing we couldn't have in Adam – the all-consuming reality of living in our Heavenly Father's love.

I've made a few pizzas in my time, but never one without any toppings – so perhaps we are at the point where the pizza analogy breaks down?

Not at all! The pizza which is 'me' is the most lavish of them all when I allow the Holy Spirit to build it. I finally find myself living according to the extravagance of the original Godly model.

My only part is to embrace the unconditional love of God as the sole object and focus of my faith, and then the Holy Spirit sets to work. He builds upon the base of the love of God (the very Bread of Life), and then the works of life which were prepared for me before the world began appear as expressions of His life, not mine.

But what would such a pizza look like? How would it differ from my life as it is now?

The toppings are no longer the diverse accumulation of all that life has placed on to me (both good and bad); they are the outcomes of the cross of Christ that have replaced my old identity in Adam. The toppings don't look like me, they look like Jesus.

We see a number of instances in the Bible where we can observe the change in thinking in the disciples as they came to terms with the extravagance of the indwelling Spirit of Jesus. Compare these contrasting accounts: In Matthew 20:23 and Mark 10:40 we read the incident where the two brothers, James and John, felt they qualified to sit at Jesus' left and right hands when He went to glory, and the other disciples where quite offended by their presumption.

After Jesus had died and risen again, and the Holy Spirit had been given to the disciples, we read two accounts in Acts 10:26 and Acts 14:15 where the apostles Peter, Paul and Barnabas were deeply troubled that certain people wanted to glorify them for their ministry; they responded with those poignant words, "We are merely men like you".

The scale and magnificence of the indwelling Spirit of God had dramatically overtaken the disciples' perspective of things; they had stepped into a completely new headspace. It was a headspace that up-valued the work of Christ so much that any earthly quality or ambition they contributed was irrelevant by comparison, and they were offended when people attempted to deflect Christ's glory onto them.

Such is the contrast between the toppings we construct and those that overflow from the Spirit of Jesus in us. But it's not a contrast between human ego and selflessness; it is a contrast between human competence and Spirit-generated life. Do you see the difference? The apostles got it; they would never use terms like 'my ministry' or 'my gifting'; it was all the expression of something bigger than themselves, and they were merely the earthly vessels that carried it around.

In the same way that John the Baptist declared, "The bride belongs to the bridegroom. The friend of the bridegroom stands and listens for him, and is overjoyed to hear the bridegroom's voice. That joy is mine, and it is now complete. *He must increase; I must decrease*" – so also we must make way for the Bridegroom (Christ), so that the Bride (the objects of His love) can be blessed by receiving directly from the source of all life.

Jesus said of John the Baptist that there was none greater than him. John was the messenger who prepared the way for the greatest event in history – yet those who followed afterwards, those who walked in the Spirit of Jesus (even the least of them), were greater than John.

That is us; we have the marvellous honour of walking around the Spirit of Jesus. If we choose to walk in the Spirit by resting in the work of the cross then we embody the greatness of the Spirit; if we choose to up-value our personal ministry or gifting in its own right, then we are limited to the flesh.

Such is the awesome capacity of the Spirit of Jesus in us,
that it can lift us out of our human competence
and into the competence of God's Spirit.

As we rest in the accomplishments of Jesus, it is as if our entire history is erased. Nothing is left of us; all the toppings that life put on us have been dismissed from their defining role, and we find ourselves topped by a new and better array of characteristics – the fruits of the Spirit of Life appear all by themselves.

CHAPTER 20

The Competence Of The Spirit

Adam redefined humanity to self-generate works of life, when we were actually designed by God to rest in His indwelling Spirit and have God generate them through us. This is not a matter of self-indulgent complacency but stepping into a source of power much bigger than ourselves. It is the mode of operation God had in mind when He conceived us.

The life of the Spirit of God working in us produces a very different result to the self-generated works we undertake. The difference is that our efforts are limited to the natural realm; they produce natural outcomes in the lives of natural people by natural means. In contrast, the outcomes produced by the Spirit of God are eternal; they are the imposition of the very life of God upon the circumstances of humanity.

The best we can do in the flesh is to help people with their physical and emotional needs, but the Spirit of God goes much deeper than that; the Holy Spirit addresses the spiritual life behind these needs and circumstances.

Jesus came that we might have Life with a capital 'L'. It's the Life that flows from the heart of God into the hearts of men and women and provides for our lives in a much deeper way than merely the provision of shelter, sustenance and emotional stability. This Life lifts us out of Adam's cycle of self, and into the circle of God's love where we discover a security far greater than the difficulties we experience in this earthly life.

And this Life flows through us too as we rest in the accomplishments of Jesus on the cross.

Let's look a little more closely at this 'resting'.

When Hebrews 4:11 says, "For whoever enters God's rest also rests from his own work, just as God did from His", it is describing a completed fact. God rested because His creation work was complete, and we are also able to rest because our total redemption from the works of Adam is complete.

All that remains is that we live in that which has been completed.

In other words, everything that was broken in Adam has now been restored in Jesus. So the important thing for us is to discover how to rest in the work that Jesus has already completed, rather than attempting to engage Him in our needs and circumstances as if His work has not been completed.

This is called faith.

> *We engage the competence of the Spirit*
> *by resting in the completed work of Jesus.*

If we are not able to rest with certainty in the accomplishments of Jesus, then we are by default resting in our own ability to get God involved by whatever means we might choose.

We gain this certainty when we determine, once and for all, that Jesus accomplished the full completion of the work He was commissioned to do – He rescued us from Satan, sin and death, He re-established our union with His Father, and gave us His righteousness and eternal divine life.

Once we have determined that this is true, we draw a line under it, step over that line, burn the old bridge back to Adam's world – and live by faith.

That faith engages the competence of the Spirit.

We are now living as spiritual beings in a natural environment. The toppings of the natural environment which previously defined us have been replaced by the life of the Spirit of Jesus, and all of the accomplishments of His cross are now our defining truth.

The Bread of Life has been topped with the Life of the Spirit.

I spent far too much of my life walking back and forth over Adam's bridge, embracing the life of the Spirit one day and mixing in my self-effort the next, never really sure that the life of the Spirit would be enough. I did it because nobody told me I could live by faith completely and for everything.

The reason for this was because nobody seemed to have actually determined what the blood of Jesus had accomplished. We knew it had fixed our sin problem, and we knew there was some Holy Spirit activity mixed in there – but we hadn't processed the completeness of it all.

It wasn't enough for me to know that Jesus had resolved my eternity and everything would be all right in the end; I needed to grasp the reality of living as a Spirit-man in eternity today. I had inadvertently assumed that the competence of the Spirit was hopefully future focussed, not assuredly present tense.

> *Religion had taught me that I was a work in progress,*
> *but the Spirit declared the opposite:*
> *I had been included in the completeness of Jesus.*

For the competency of the Holy Spirit to be operational in my life, I needed to rest in my completeness in Christ instead of my incompleteness in Adam. I needed to determine once and for all that I sat at the banquet table of God's love as Jesus, and that the legacy of Adam no longer existed for me.

My competency to walk through life by faith is 'as Christ'; I can rest in the Father's love as the source of my life as if I am Jesus Himself (which I am by His indwelling).

I just made a statement which is beyond our wildest imagination – yet it rolls off the tongue as if it is just another clever Christian cliché. This statement transforms my meagre earthly competence into the extraordinary supernatural competence of the Spirit of Jesus. It is the ultimate divine topping exchange.

> *My new toppings are not me – they are Jesus.*

The next chapter should have no words in it so there is nothing to compete with the immeasurable truth you have just read, so take your time to let it sink in before we go on.

CHAPTER 21
To Be Christian

As I reviewed my Christian walk over a lifetime, I had to admit to myself that the greater part of it was not lived 'as Christ'. Instead it was 'me' being the best version of me that I could come up with at the time, given my circumstances and personality, etc.

In a comparative sense I was doing okay living out my days as a responsible Christian husband, father and business man. Some people did better than I and some not as well, but in the end we were all defined by one thing – we were managing life as best we could with what we had.

There were times when I pondered whether I was actually Christian at all back then because the change in me has been so radical that I feel like I have been born again… *again.* Yet the potential of the work of the cross to transform my spirit is not limited by my ability to see the truth clearly; it is all the gift of God through Christ, for which I am eternally grateful. Jesus renewed my spirit long ago, in spite of me; and I have just begun to see it.

At the age of 55 I began to see Jesus as I had never seen Him before and now, 10 years later, I understand a little more still, and the thing that continues to unfold is that it's all about Jesus, not me.

If you've been around Christian circles even a little bit, that last statement – "it's all about Jesus" –will not be unfamiliar. It pops up most Sundays and attracts the usual chorus of "amens".

But what exactly does it mean?

In what way exactly is it "all about Jesus"? The answer makes it the statement that defines what it is to be Christian.

Here are a few possibilities:

He is the best example of a life well lived for us to model ourselves upon.

He is the motivator of my ministry, service or passion.

We have built the Christian faith around His message of love and sacrifice.

I try to keep my thoughts on Him and meditate on Him all day.

He is the one who binds us all together in the community of the church.

He gives my life purpose, meaning and direction.

I love to worship Him and sense His presence and power.

He is the central figure of human history who defines my life.

Up until the age of fifty-five, when my life was shaken up by the pressures of business, I had been happy with those answers. It was not until the foundations of my life were shaken to the core that I got around to examining the substance of these statements and considering afresh what it actually is to be Christian.

Upon closer analysis, I realised that those answers were all about me, not Jesus. And even though I had collected all of those statements under the umbrella of 'it's all about Jesus', that didn't make it so. They were actually statements about my expression, my sense of purpose, and my need for meaning – they were all about me.

And very slowly, as I began to unpack my Christianity over several years, I started to see something I hadn't seen before in all the time I had been a Christian. Jesus didn't come to give me purpose or meaning or expression; He came to give me Himself.

To be Christian is to have Christ.

Did I have Christ before the age of fifty-five? Absolutely, but He was so hidden in my purpose, meaning and expression that I hardly noticed Him there. So my quest became one of discovering the meaning of the statement, 'Jesus came to give me Himself' without all the competing din of my self-oriented worldview.

The first hurdle was to determine if there was actually enough left in my Christianity after sidelining my need for purpose, meaning and expression for me to build my identity around. In other words, what would a form of Christianity that was 'all about Jesus' actually look like?

Initially I thought it would be a bit spartan and bland, that it would be lacking life and colour if all I had was Christ, because up until that time the life and colour had come from me, and my engagement in all the stuff of Christianity.

So I pondered what it would be like if my Christianity contained only Jesus and me.

Could I survive in such a stripped back type of faith?

And who would I be if I did – what would be left of me?

And the biggest question of all – did I actually want a Christianity that just had Christ?

As I pondered these questions, my thoughts went to Paul and the long period of time he spent in the wilderness of life before he embarked on his ministry and missionary trips. I wondered if he needed to work this through as well, that he needed to empty himself of his extensive resume of self-defining truths in order to lay hold of the one great truth he really needed: the surpassing greatness of knowing Christ. And that Christ could not be truly known through our need for purpose, meaning and expression; He could only be known by our personal discovery of the fact that at His cross He gave us Himself.

> *To be Christian is to have Christ,*
> *not to do Christian things.*

If you've read any of my earlier books, you will probably be aware that at this point in time I asked God to show me Jesus. I have to admit upon reflection that it is a sad state of affairs that a person who has been actively engaged in the Christian life for fifty-five years needs to ask God a question like that – that we seem to have collectively skipped over 'having Christ' so that we could get on with our need for purpose, meaning and expression.

At the time I didn't know if that question was important, but it must have been because God responded beyond my wildest expectations.

CHAPTER 22

To Have Christ

Once I dialled down the din of my personal need for purpose, meaning and expression, I began to see some things that were so superior to it, that a whole new form of Christianity began to take shape.

This new form of Christianity contained just one thing – Jesus.

But it was a different Jesus than I had ever known before; it was a Jesus who was enough in Himself. He didn't need to be contained in my need for purpose, meaning and expression because He filled every part of me with Himself quite apart from my purpose, meaning and expression.

His love for me was enough.

My need for purpose, meaning and expression was not bad in itself, but it had a way of competing with Jesus for His enough-ness. It had a way of defining me, when only the love of God was truly able to do that.

As I dialled down all the purpose, meaning and expression, I found myself overwhelmed by the scale of God's extravagant love. It was the difference between a bleak overcast day, and a bright sunny day. The light and love of God started to get into me and fill me and warm me. It was there all along, but all the purpose, meaning and expression seemed to screen me from it, such that the real thing that Jesus came to do was unable to reach me.

In one sense I began to discover a new kind of self-indulgence that God wanted for me – not a preoccupation with myself, but a willingness to let myself be loved by God for His reasons, not mine.

This ability to let myself be loved by God without the addition of my need for purpose, meaning and expression has liberated me to the freedom of knowing Christ. It was God's idea all along that I would be carried through life by His great love, and the self-indulgence of knowing Christ (just because I can) has resulted in a sense of completeness bigger than me.

> *I was designed by God to indulge in His great love.*

As I went along, it became clear that much of my engagement in purpose, meaning and expression was my way of compensating for the fact that I didn't know how to let God love me, *or if I was even allowed to indulge in His love.* It required a complete review of my reason for being here to get this sorted out. It was part of the shuffling process; I needed to determine for myself what was the primary fact of my existence and shuffle it to the top of the pile.

> *Only one card could be at the top:*
> *my purpose, meaning and expression*
> *or my identity as the object of God's love.*

That may not seem like such a big thing to many readers because we all acknowledge that we are nothing without God. But I am talking about something far greater than merely assigning to God my headship and supreme authority from which is motivated my purpose, meaning and expression; I am saying that God has no interest in my purpose, meaning and expression if I have not first indulged in His great love for me.

And so began my indulgent life.

But a disclaimer before we go on: it was not primarily related to material or physical things; it was an indulgence in the heart of God, not His capacity to meet my earthly needs.

I live in the southern part of the Australian mainland. Sometimes we have four seasons in one day, and we certainly experience diversity in our weather and enjoy the distinction of the changing seasons. We have family in Sydney whose weather is more predictable, and one sunny day after another rolls by, so much so that they have little awareness of the changing seasons. Our Sydney relatives just anticipate that one day will be like the next – it is just where they live. That is what is normal for them.

It is this expectation that God's love will always be shining on my life that best defines this new understanding of Christianity – I now live in a place where His love fills me and warms me every day. The reality of that love is quite apart from my circumstances; it's not about that – it's not a question of whether God has moved into my world and repaired my earthly life, but whether Jesus has moved me into His world where the environment of God's love fills everything.

So now I live as a citizen of heaven; it is my new home. I live there because Jesus gave me Himself, and that is where He lives. I don't wonder if God's love will shine on me from one day to the next because I have discovered that His love always reaches those who live in His home – it is just where they live.

And I indulge in that love because I have realised that it is His desire and plan that I would. I don't try to convince God to do anything; He is already fully convinced to shower His love upon me because it is inherent in His nature to do that – so I simply live in it confidently.

>   ***My indulgent life is His idea not mine.***

Overflowing from this indulgence may come many different forms of service and ministry, but they come simply because His life in me wells up and bubbles over. I am simply the earthen vessel that holds His great love.

I use the word *indulgent* because it conveys such a contrast to our normal thinking. It implies a willingness on God's part, and more than that, an expectation and anticipation that we will revel in His love. He is at last able to be true to His divine nature when we allow Him to saturate us in His love (just because He can).

His love makes its home in us as we shift our security away from purpose, meaning and expression and onto the great act of love Jesus expressed on the cross. That is the environment that His love flourishes in, and we partake in it by resting there.

The love of God has a remarkable capacity to hold us that we cannot obtain from any earthly comparison; it is so extravagantly liberating that all we need to do is grasp the extraordinary nature of it and cast our entire existence into it.

There is no qualification, hesitation or preparation; we simply step into it and let it enfold us for what it is – the most lavish and real fact of our lives. I am qualified because Jesus carries me in, I am there in the Father's presence in Christ, and in as true a way as Christ is Himself. If I hesitate to bathe in God's love, then I diminish the ability of the blood of Jesus to carry me there. If I shore up my insecurity with various religious or lifestyle preparations, then I am effectively discounting the efficacy of Jesus sacrifice.

Jesus came to give me Himself, and I am choosing to have Him.

CHAPTER 23

Will The Real Graeme Please Stand Up

It's been a few chapters since we made use of the pizza metaphor, so allow me to draw a distinction between the toppings that we bring to the Bread of Life, and the toppings that the Holy Spirit brings. In ourselves we bring the best of Adam. That may sound a bit harsh because our intentions and motivations are good and well-intended, but the fact remains that all we have to offer is the best of humanity unless we come as Christ. When we lean in to the love of God expressed on the cross, things work differently; the Holy Spirit brings the life of Christ into everything we do.

You might be thinking that the Holy Spirit is automatically present in all we do simply by virtue of the fact that we are Christians, but that is not the case. It comes down to whether we actually embrace and trust in the work of the cross as our source of life. It is about faith, not merely participation.

> *To have the Holy Spirit's works of life expressed in my life,
> I must decide once and for all who I am.*

I must decide if I am ready to step away from all the earthly props that have supported me thus far and hide myself in the work of Jesus for my entire sense of worth and identity. I must decide if my life is safe in Him and that He is enough for me in every regard for the Holy Spirit to freely flow through me. There can be no hidden rooms or inaccessible compartments in our lives; we must trust Jesus with everything, because if we don't trust Him with everything, we are effectively trusting Him with nothing.

This is a different ball game from going to church, being involved in the various programs, and learning to speak the language – this is the end of our life as we know it. It is being in a quiet room with Jesus only, nobody else is present – and declaring loud and clear that He is my life, I have entrusted every fibre of my being into His care.

> *I cannot fool Jesus and I cannot fool myself…*
> *this is the end.*

If we are unable to do that, then we will continue to bring the best of Adam to all we put your hands to. The best of Adam is not so bad; he was as good as a man can be – but he had stepped out of his love union with God.

If I choose to hide myself in the work of Christ in this way, then a new man appears on the stage. He is a man who is so filled with the life of Christ that for all intents and purposes they are inseparable. They might look different on the outside, but on the inside they are both energized and given life directly from the heart of God.

> *The real me stands up when I choose to believe this,*
> *I am the man that Jesus remade.*

I had previously thought that Jesus inhabited my individual activities, that he responded to my efforts to bring change, healing, and restoration, and engaged in them in partnership with me. Now I understand that He inhabits me, and His Spirit takes over everything – I no longer live, but Christ lives in me.

So it's not so much about my availability, but whether I have grasped the scale of His great love and hidden my existence in it. In the past we used to bandy around the clever line, "It's not about your ability, but your availability" – but even availability doesn't cut it if we have not first grasped the spectacle which is the love of God.

My availability, purpose, meaning and expression is not the real me in Christ; that is the old me in Adam. The real me has seen something so far beyond human capability that it abandons all alternatives in a heartbeat to have the real thing.

Viewing the scale of the love of God will do that to you.

> **Something finally registers
> that there is something bigger than me going on here.**

That God is more than theology, He is more than my engagement with the community that bears His name – He is supremely loving, and I am the object and focus of that love. My old Adamic thinking wants to hold God in a more manageable form. It wants God to be measured like me – but He is off the scale and His love is too. We just need to open our eyes and see it.

I know a man who mentors some of the young guys in the church he attends; he attempts to encourage and help them in their faith, and life in general. I appreciate his good intentions, but I am troubled by the perspective of God that he passes on to these young men. He tells them that it is hard to have faith, and that to hope to know God is very unrealistic and an inexact science, so the best thing to do is accept the theology of Him and get on with life in the church.

Little does he know that he is robbing these young men of the adventure of a lifetime.

They need to be told that God is as real as they are, even more real, and that His love is the most profoundly dependable fact of their lives. He needs to raise the bar instead of lowering it and speak of the extravagance of knowing and being known by God. *What a waste!* What a tragedy that a Christian mentor is happy to hold his pupils in the legacy of Adam.

What a sad state of affairs that willing young men are presented with such a pared back view of God that He bears no actual resemblance to the true scale and nature of who He really is. These young men are being discouraged from standing up and being themselves.

"Will the real Graeme please stand up?" He can only stand up if Graeme knows who he really is; otherwise Graeme will stand up as Adam.

Here lies the challenge for all of us. Will we embrace the claims of God as our life-defining truth, or will we hold Him in our theological folder? Because if the claims He makes about the scale and nature of His love for humanity are true, then it would be madness for us to live as if they are merely hopeful speculation.

The middle ground of my mentor friend doesn't work. God is either the extravagantly loving and good God He claims to be, or He is an idol invented by Adam's self-obsessed imagination. God has put His love on display for us on the cross of Christ; it is in the public domain – and we are now invited to live in it, be held in place by it, and walk through life in the confident security of it.

This is true Christianity.

The blinkers of Adam's small thinking attempt to conceal this from us; they attempt to block out the greater part of our lavish union with God and leave us wallowing in the mediocrity of Adam's narrow view. We were not designed by God to live in this narrow space; it is not who we are. We were designed to walk out to the extremities of God's goodness, not be confined within the limitations of uncertainty.

Jesus removed the blinkers of Adam's small thinking and exposed us once again to the infinite vista of God's unthinkable love for us. That is why He came, so that we could see a panoramic view of the true heart of God, and in seeing it, choose it as our place of habitation.

That is the 'life' that Jesus came to give.

CHAPTER 24

Extravagance

On some level, all Christians acknowledge the extravagant nature of God; He is clearly bigger than us.

Very often, though, our perception of the vast extravagance of God is contained within our small earthly concepts. We imagine God in human terms because we have no other material to work with. We don't deliberately box God in, and we don't realize that we perceive Him through the lens of Adam's small thinking; we just don't instinctively get the scale of what we are in.

There is only one way to expand our thinking out to its true proportions. We must spend time considering the cross of Christ – it contains the expression on earth of all that is embodied in the vast nature of God.

The cross of Christ is normalized in the thinking of many Christians. We acknowledge that it is the greatest event in history, but we don't know how to lift it out of history and into the present where it can be examined and owned for what it truly is.

I will try and lift it out of history for you now:

Imagine if you won a competition to accompany John and Jackie Kennedy in the open top limousine as it toured the streets of Dallas on that fateful day when John F. Kennedy, the president of the free world, was assassinated. Fifty years later, it would be an historic event; but as far as you are concerned, it is part of your reality because you were there when it happened – you were part of it all. For you, it would be more than an event that took place in JFK's life. It would also be an event that took place in your life.

Now imagine that the bullet that passed through JFK's head, continued on and passed through your head; imagine you were included in the assassination of the President of America. You are now inextricably a participant in this momentous, world-changing event. You are not part of the general population that watched it from the sidewalks, or stared in disbelief at the television, or read about it years later; you were there, and you experienced exactly the same death as JFK.

This event has captured the attention of every generation that followed; it has generated an extensive list of books, theories and conclusions, and still today is the subject of ongoing speculation. But for you, none of that matters because the enormity of that event has already defined you. You were not an observer or commentator – you were in it.

As far as you are concerned John F. Kennedy did not merely give his life for the cause of the free world; he pulled you into that cause by including you in his death – and now the whole terrible thing is as real and defining for you as it is for him.

Although you have lived for many years and days leading up to this event, although you have experienced a great deal before this moment, none of that defines you any longer – you are now contained and defined by this one fact: you died with JFK. It is as if all that went before was swallowed up in time, and you became defined by a completely different and foreign reality. All you wanted was to go on a joyride with the main man. There was no mention of his cause, or connection between his life and yours… but you found yourself caught up in his death anyway.

I know that it is a stretch to get you to see yourself in the event of JFK's assassination because you weren't really there, but it does serve to illustrate an event that we were in – the event of the crucifixion of Jesus.

> *The enormity of Christ's death defines you,*
> *what Christ experienced in the body*
> *you experienced in the spirit.*

Our natural tendency, to see the event of Jesus' death and resurrection as a point in history when certain religious outcomes were accomplished, is a seriously incomplete view of things. Even outcomes as important as the payment of the penalty due to us for the sins we have committed barely covers the scale of it, because it was more than the payment of a penalty. It was the inclusion of our Adamic nature in that death.

Jesus went to the cross as the last Adam; He took the entire human race onto the cross in His body, and we were all killed there with Him. Every one of us was mysteriously crucified with Christ. The symbolic bullet that killed Jesus also killed the nature of Adam in all of us.

This catastrophic annihilation of the descendants of Adam was absolutely completed on the cross; no one survived. When Jesus was buried, so was every human being who ever lived; not one living person was left on planet earth. As far as God was concerned, the human race ceased to exist when it was crucified with Christ.

It was the end.

Then after three days Jesus burst out of the grave; death could not hold Him. His resurrection was so all-powerful that He destroyed death, as well as sin.

When Jesus rose from the dead, the most remarkable phenomenon took place. Dead men and women began to open their eyes too; they began standing up and walking around as a completely new race of human beings. They had become human beings that had been given the right to be the sons and daughters of God.

1 Corinthians 15:22 says, "For as in Adam all die, so in Christ all will be made alive".

These men and women had no understanding of what had happened; they didn't realise that they had just participated in the greatest event in history. They didn't feel the nails driven through their hands and feet. They didn't feel anything. They thought it was all just a great big theological story – because it had all taken place in the invisible realm of the Spirit.

But over time, a very long time, these men and women began to see the truth. They began to understand that they had been through death – and so they embraced this new life that came from Jesus.

The reason they began to understand this is because the Holy Spirit showed them something beyond their natural sight; He showed them the truth as God sees it – that Jesus had carried them into His grave and His resurrection from it, and that His life was now theirs for the taking because the nature of Adam was dead. There was no impediment to this new life but for their choice to have it. They didn't need to wait till they died, because they had already died with Christ – all they had to do was say "thanks".

To be killed with another person is a very defining thing. It has a way of focussing our attention away from all of the toppings of Christianity and onto the one fact that makes us Christian. It gives us the opportunity to rethink things so that we step back from the very broad view of Christianity and focus in on the narrow view – the single fact that we were crucified with Christ.

> **I participated in exactly the same death as Jesus.**

The broader joy ride of Christianity is now irrelevant, because the whole terrible thing that happened to Jesus has caught hold of me too.

Was that cruel? Was that a nasty act that God allowed Jesus to pull me into His death?

Quite the opposite is true; it was the most extravagant expression of God's love for me possible. Something was going on in the death of Jesus that was beyond mere benevolence, beyond saving us because no one else could – it was the heart of God laid bare.

God knew better than I did; He could see through the whole good and evil joy ride that Adam's family were stuck in. It had given us the false sense of security that only a ride in an open top limousine can give – *that the world around us was just as it seemed.*

But the world wasn't just as it seemed… and God loved us too much to allow us to stay in it.

When Adam took leave of the environment of God's love, he created a false sense of security to replace that environment. He created a world view which validated us by our management of the toppings (good and evil), and in so doing he reduced the extravagance of God down to a similarly manageable scale.

The most loving thing God could do for us was to remove us from that false environment – even though we are so attached to it. The most loving thing God could do was to relocate us back into the environment of His gloriously extravagant love and goodness.

Adam invented a new way to have God's love based on how well we are doing with our toppings, and religion has unknowingly perpetuated Adam's way because it has lost sight of the true blazing spectacle which is our God of love. It reduced God to the smallness of conditional love, a love that we purchase with our religious and lifestyle personal best.

What a God! What amazing love, that He has pulled us out of our false world by including us in the death of His dear Son, Jesus.

What an amazing thing it is to know that there is something greater than what we can see, and that we have been pulled into it by love. The unfolding discovery of this greater realm is now our quest and obsession – *but what could be greater than our familiar world?*

It must be beyond our wildest dreams.

CHAPTER 25
Wildest Dreams

At times it can be hard to see through all the toppings of Christianity and get a proper view of the extravagance of God's love – our careful management of all that is good, and our stand against all that is evil, has a way of filling our screen. It's hard to imagine that there could be more than that – that a form of Christianity awaits us which is so far beyond our limited perspective that it exceeds our wildest dreams.

Jesus and His Father live in this place beyond our wildest dreams, and Jesus gave His life to take us back there. It is not the small place that Adam led us to believe it was; it is unthinkably extravagant in every possible way. To think that God could somehow be compressed into religion is the height of Adam's folly.

Human language, and my ability to make use of it, are incapable of describing the world that Jesus knows. The difference when we compare black and white to technicolour might go some of the way, but I think the best we can do is use the comparison that Jesus used Himself – the difference between death and life.

Death is 'us in Adam'. It is us in our management of good and evil. It is us presenting God with our personal best in lifestyle and religion (the best toppings we can come up with) in the hope of attracting His pleasing response. Every one of us, even the very best of us who ever lived, are miserably lost in this terrible condition of death.

We just don't know it;
we don't know that the world is not what it seems.

The apostle John made it clear in John 6:63 when he said, "The Spirit gives life, the flesh counts for nothing".

Jesus came to give the walking dead the life of heaven. He killed death in us and exposed us to a life so divine, so pure, and so all-encompassing, that it rendered our toppings to be nothing more than the dim glow of a flickering candle compared to the blazing glow of the sun.

We have been attached to that flickering candle for too long; it's been the death of us to try to live well enough to please God, when there isn't actually any Godly goodness in us. It's time to stop trying and to abandon ourselves to the blazing love of God.

Unlike death, life is living every moment of every day in the blazing glory of God's extravagant love. We were designed for this freely given love, it is the source of all that we need, and it was so intrinsically in the heart of God when He conceived humanity that, as far as He is concerned, to live without it is to be dead.

So when Jesus declared in John 10:10 that the reason He came was that we might have life, and have it abundantly, He was referring to giving our 'dead to God' spirits the kiss of life – in other words, the purpose of the cross is that He would return us to the environment of God's love.

In ancient times, long, long before God had spoken anything into existence, He dreamed His wildest dream. It was a dream that was so extravagant, and so staggeringly divine, that it was like a river of love bursting forth from His innermost being – the ultimate expression of the full measure of the heart of God.

And this dream came true in you and me.

God dreamed His most extravagant dream, and it was me. The greatest expression of the greatest love in all eternity was God's love for me.

It was all of us, but I cannot personalize it for anyone else – each one of us must say "it was for me".

I am the one God loves.

He has had me in His heart long before Adam breathed his first breath, even before the first ray of light escaped from the first star that was catapulted into the heavens by His word. Long before then His love knew me.

And when Adam wandered away from this love, God did not falter. He did not reconsider or question His decision to love us, because God's love for us was not in any way governed by Adam's actions. It was instead determined in the ancient days of eternity and would blaze on for all eternity; God would always be true to Himself.

According to the book of Revelation, Jesus is the Lamb that was slain before the world began. The death and resurrection of Jesus was not God's Plan B because Plan A did not work out. God had counted the cost of my salvation long before He began to create anything – He knew the beginning to the end and never for a second doubted His decision to create me from His love.

That's what makes God's dream of humanity so wild… *He knew.*

That's what makes God's extravagant love so certain… He knew all our days, all the good and evil, and He didn't even blink. Such is this ancient love that has held me from eternity to eternity.

God's wildest dream and my wildest dream coincided on the cross of Jesus. The ancient longing within me to be loved without any strings attached, and the ancient truth about God that I would be the object of His wild love, became one magnificent reality when Jesus cried out, "It is finished". At last the circle was closed, the heart-longing of the Creator and the created were satisfied for all eternity – because it was God's design that I would know Him as He really is.

In my opinion, the apostle Paul has come closest in expressing the magnificence of this love, as he crafted human language around it in Ephesians 3:14-19: "For this reason I kneel before the Father, from whom every family in heaven and on earth derives its name. I pray that out of His glorious riches He may strengthen you with power through His Spirit in your inner being, so that Christ may dwell in your hearts through faith. And I pray that you, being rooted and established in love, may have power, together with all the Lord's holy people, to grasp how wide and long and high and deep is the love of Christ, and to know this love that surpasses knowledge – that you may be filled to the measure of all the fullness of God".

Wow, it leaves you a bit short of breath. It's like the heart of God has swept down low and touched me with the truth and given me a glimpse into the wildest dream ever conceived, and I can feel it completing and filling me, like I have never been filled before.

This wild dream holds me in a way I have never known before – continually held in place, filled, nourished and warmed by its unrelenting radiant love.

This love is just like the earth is to the sun, held in place by the staggering pull of the sun's gravity so that the radiance of the sun's glow can give life, nourishment and warmth. That is me; held in place by the strong love of God – and as I rest in the pull of His love, I find that I am also filled, nourished and warmed by it.

> *God holds me in His love so that He can give me His life…*
> *that is perfection!*

Adam thought his deeds could hold him in place, but how wrong he was. His deeds were no more capable of holding him in place than the gravity from a flickering candle could hold the earth in place; there was no chance. Yet Adam made a religion out of trying.

> *Each of us must decide for ourselves what will hold us in place;*
> *no one else can decide for us.*

Adam made the wrong choice, and the human race was defined by that choice for a very long time.

Now Jesus has given us the choice again… the choice to let the love of God be enough.

Cheers,

Graeme

www.ingramcontent.com/pod-product-compliance
Lightning Source LLC
Chambersburg PA
CBHW072100290426
44110CB00014B/1759